On the End Times

Or

The First Return of Christ

Jacques Cabaud

**En Route Books & Media, LLC
St. Louis, MO, USA**

⊕ENROUTE
Make the time

En Route Books and Media, LLC
5705 Rhodes Avenue
St. Louis, MO 63109

Cover credit: TJ Burdick

Library of Congress Control Number: 2018960337

ISBN-13: 978-1-7325949-9-9
ISBN-10: 1-7325949-9-6

DEDICATION

To my physician, Dr. Maria Diepgen, without whose professional help, this book would not have seen the light day.

EPIGRAPHS

"You heard me say to you: 'I go away, and I will come to you.'" (Jn 14, 28)

"The Lord is near." (Phil 4, 5)

"Be patient... for the coming of the Lord is at hand." (James 5, 8)

"For yet a very little while, he who is to come, will come, and will not delay." (Heb 10,37)

"The words of the true one, who has the key of David, who opens and no one shall shut, who shuts and no one opens...: 'I am coming soon.'" (Apoc 3, 7 & 11)

"Thus Christ, having been offered once to bear the sins of many, will appear a second time, not to deal with sin but to save those who are eagerly waiting for him." (Heb 9, 28)

Nota Bene—As the Bible most fitting to the occasion, I chose for the quotations the Challoner-Rheims, the King James, or the Standard Revised versions (RSV, Oxford, 2002)—or even tried to improve upon them. Of course, the ultimate authority in terms of meaning remains the versions approved by the Church. The acronym used for the Apocalypse will be "Ap" or "Apoc".

The following text was first conceived as a series of lectures, hence at times the colloquial tone.

I was not trying to read in the future. I meant to bring together all the information available from the various sources at my disposal.

The future only makes sense once it is with us—except in the light of a Faith enlightened by the gift of prophecy.

Dear Reader, may I draw your attention to the footnotes. In the main text, I express my ideas; in the footnotes, I present the facts on which these ideas are based. And what is a thesis without the data upon which it rests as on the solid foundation of reality?

This is the book of a true son of the Church.
If some formulations are hazardous,
Or some mistakes were made, I regret them.
Far from superfluous disputes,
I have tried to foster a spirit of discernment.

CONTENTS

PREFACE

We all know that there will be a Last Judgment. This does not mean that this is the only Judgment to be expected. As the past shows, God punishes those whom he loves, as parents do with a child for his own benefit. God in his Fatherhood always has the good of all his creatures in mind, the highest of which for rational creatures is their ability to love Him and each other through Him.

When Adam and Eve exchanged this divine faculty, initially to satisfy a concupiscent urge and conclusively as a surge of pride, they lost the fullness of their birthright. The return to the fullness of Sonship would be a long and arduous task; and the world having drowned in sin in the days of Noah, a new beginning had to be made. As for the Jewish people, they were chastised by exile in an exemplary way when they strayed.

The New Testament was no less explicit in its teaching on the consequences of sin. Providential justice is not arbitrary: it affects history. Absolute Justice, because it is timeless, is not of this world. Hell or Heaven are forever. Relative justice, on the other hand, is of this world. The lazy man cannot reap the fruit of his labors since there are hardly any. The drunkard cannot take for granted his liver's ability to dispose of the sequels of his drinking. Farniente Southern Italians unwittingly hand over the keys of their economy to the Mafia.

i

It is Christ who tells us that virtue reaps a hundred fold in this life and eternal bliss in the other. On the collective level, the fall of empires follows upon the apex of their expansion. At its height, the Roman Empire numbered sixty million inhabitants; in its final stage, thirty million.

A historical evolution can no less be foretold, at least in retrospect. Had Hitler overcome his anti-Semitic prejudice, Germany would have retained its leading Jewish scientists, such as Einstein, and been the first country to build what was at the time the absolute weapon: the atomic bomb. Russia had an expanding economy when Lenin destroyed private property. In spite of state controlled industry, it could not feed its own population in the early thirties, nor without American lend-lease resist an aggressive Germany.

As for our modern World, it is living above its means in the more advanced nations, heaping debt upon debt for future generations to settle. The very burden of monies due will weigh upon our children as a threat of inflation. We treat the problem as if it would vanish by itself. The plight of contemporary Greece could be ours, all of us, one day, but without wealthier fellow-countries to rescue us from disaster. Such is the bitter fruit of lack of foresight.

The sufferings brought about by the collapse of this one-world economy cannot be equally distributed. This could lead those countries with the mightiest armies to settle things to their advantage by war. Conflicts have been generated on lesser grounds in the past. The difference is that the means of destruction are such today that they imperil the very survival of mankind. Providence needs no other excuse to intervene and set things right through the forthcoming Parousia, or Judgment of Nations. As we should have learned from the story of Jonah, prophecies usually have a hypothetical character. The reason is simple: if people believe a disaster will happen as the inevitable result of their sins, the foretold event will not necessarily take place since men can make amends for their wrongdoings and reform before the foretold event takes place. This proves that belief in prophecy affects the future favorably.

This point once established, the purpose of our book should be a tribute to optimism. Bad news concerning the future is good news if, as with the Nineveh of Jonah, it brings about the contrary of what had been expected. This is why a prophetic book—or even a mere compendium of prophetic writings—may be considered uplifting literature and have a positive impact on the morale, not to mention the morality, of its readers.

In the light of this "art of positive thinking," this opus of mine will hopefully fulfill the purpose for which it was written. It is as prophetic as can be, given my sources of information which are the Bible, Tradition, Mystics, and Visionaries of all times.

Prophecies are to be taken seriously. Those of Fatima prove this point. Once the Church started acting upon the demands made upon it by Heaven, events turned to the advantage of mankind: the Wall dividing Western Europe fell as if by magic.

When Heaven speaks, should we not listen?

Once Pope John Paul II had consecrated officially the world and implicitly Russia to the Immaculate Heart of Mary, we realized that Heaven kept its part of the conditional promises it made. To be precise, the consecration of the world was made by Pope John Paul II in a loud voice—and that of Russia in a whisper for prudential diplomatic reasons.

In France we say: "Un homme prévenu en vaut deux." Loosely translated, this means that once we have been forewarned, we are far more likely to make the right decisions.

This is the theory. What is the practice?

We had been told at Fatima (1917) that if men carried on as in the past the future would be bleak. And such has been the case. Mankind had not learned the lesson to be drawn from World War I, which is that sin engenders war as an effect flows from its cause.

Heaven respects the laws registered in the nature of things: "necessity rules our ends." This saying of Shakespeare does not deny the part played by human liberty in the making of history. It means that the misuse of the divinely granted attribute of freedom places mankind under the rule of the law according to which evil promotes evil.

Sin generates conflict.

In other words, not only is virtue its own reward, but it also turns to the advantage of the virtuous. It pays to be good.

Heaven keeps telling us: "If you do not repent, you shall die." Death had been foretold to Adam and Eve before they ate of the forbidden fruit. They ate of it notwithstanding and found out to their dismay that henceforth they would be defenseless against "the stings of nature": they were naked, and they would age until their bodies turned to dust. Concupiscence would prey on man as the serpent had done in Paradise.

Whether they liked it or not, they would have to pay the price for sin. One of these consequences was hell for whoever behaved like Cain, in defiance of the sacredness of life. The harmony between God's will and man's freedom had been broken. Return to primeval innocence would be a long and tedious process, and only partially successful.

It would seem out of reach for man seen on the collective level. (Detailed information on this very point will be found in this book.)

As history deals with the past, so does prophecy with the future. But in a different way. While history records what has taken place in such a manner that it cannot be changed, prophecy announces what should happen, according to our own use or misuse of freedom.

The past is motionless, the future is conditional—at least for those factors that depend upon our own decisions. A prophecy is a warning. For its interpretation, a charism is needed, no less a gift than that of prophecy. "Who receives a prophet as a prophet, deserves a prophet's due." He who writes on prophecies builds a bridge between prophecies and those to whom they are addressed.

In this case, however, as happens when a text is translated, communication introduces, just like with translation, an element of subjectivity. One of the author's most obvious handicaps will be his attempt to fit a variety of elements into a coherent whole.

There is a warning Christ made to a mystic concerning the wish to know the day of one's own death: "If everyone knew it, few would be saved." This uncertainty is one of the psychological needs of the soul. Once again, "readiness is all." To live is to take a risk. It does not pertain to mankind to know its future as it does its past.

Nonetheless, prophecy does help to meet the challenge of forthcoming events. Trust in Providence is required; and this trust finds its expression in the practice of virtue. In the meantime, we can only conjecture on the basis of what prophets have told us.

We see the future within the boundaries of conceivable possibilities. Inferences can be drawn, but only up to a certain point. Thus, in this book, I preferred loose-ends to an artificial harmony and tried to respect whatever uncertainties remained.

At this point, Léon Bloy's cautionary comment is appropriate: "Of all human faculties, memory is that which was most affected by the Fall [of our first parents]. A most certain proof of the infirmity of our memory is our ignorance of the future."

When Christ was crucified against the all too human expectations of the Apostles, their resulting confusion rested on the selective role of wishful thinking. They had not registered the information offered by Christ's prophecies concerning His own death and Resurrection.

If we do not intend to stumble as they had, let us take into serious consideration what we have been told by Messengers from Heaven concerning the eschatological Passion and Resurrection of our Mother the Church, patterned somewhat on those of Christ himself, while we follow the guidelines she proposes for speculation.

While men realize only too well that the seed of the future is sown in the present, they have trouble conceiving what will become of this world several generations from now.

This restriction, however, does not affect in the same way what we call scientific fiction and mere daydreaming. That flying would not always be restricted to birds was a gleam in the eyes of Da Vinci. Archimedes (287-212 BC) had already built a mirror that could focus into one beam the light of the sun to set wooden ships on fire. We do so today in the Mojave desert to produce electricity. There is a logic in material progress, if we only respect the conditions necessary for its development.

That is why we give credence to what would be inconceivable otherwise. And when we read that St. Nilus, as early as in the fifth century (+430), announced that one day men would fly, explore the depths of the sea, travel at unheard-of velocity, and instantly communicate with one another from one end of the world to the other, we take it for granted that he was a sage of sorts. There is a plausibility in dreams based on an exponential increase of technical possibilities.

What makes us pause is that this visionary Saint related

these positive achievements to concur with disquieting changes in human behavior, especially in the areas we ascribe to what we call today "gender ideology." He tells us that women will dress up like men, and vice-versa, and since appearance impacts on comportment, a reversal of roles will ensue.

This state of affairs will not only give the lie to customary habits, it will nurture new norms of morality—if there is such a thing—in our society. Based on State intervention, what was considered immoral will to a large extent be considered legal to the extent that "murder at home," according to St. Nilus, will be permissible, doubtless under the guise of abortion or euthanasia. He was not specific on this point, but after the fact, we can be.

Briefly stated, St. Nilus issues the warning that when aberration is considered the norm, the Antichrist is nigh. He, the fourth century anchorite, writes as a prophet, as many other visionaries after him. He even goes out on a limb when he mentions dates: "...Towards the middle of the 20th century, people... will become unrecognizable. As the time of the coming of the Antechrist approaches, the intelligence of men will be darkened by carnal passions..."[1]

We tend to pass off as part and parcel of human Psyche its present obsession with sex without realizing that this cultural bias is fairly recent. In 1900, all Christian denominations, including the Jews, were in agreement with Tradition concerning what was morally permissible in the area of sexual morality. The dam broke first at the Lambeth conference of the Anglican Church in 1930, with the claim of absolute primacy for the individual conscience. The other

---

1 For the quotes and the information concerning St. Nilus, see Jean Mathiot in *L'Antéchrist et l'Antichrist*" (Ohnet-le-Château, Rassemblement à son Image, pp. 30-32).

Protestant denominations soon followed suit. To this trend, the Encyclicals of Paul VI, John-Paul II and Benedict XVI stand as lone bastions of resistance.

St. Nilus is but one of many prophets underlining the contrast between material progress and moral decay that is to reach its peak in the "Endtimes." His dating of forthcoming events is all the more worth mentioning since he is speaking about us and condemning our ways...

Since his days, many voices have been raised similarly in warning. Well worth mentioning is Jean de Vézelay, or John of Jerusalem (1042-1119), a Templar Crusader who liberated that town from the Turks in 1099. During his stay in Palestine, he wrote a "Secret protocol of prophecies" in two parts.

The First part deals with the beginning years of the XXth century, and the second one announces an "era of confidence, faith and hope" as a living contrast to the previous period of sin and confusion.[2]

> I. – Jerusalem will fall under Jewish control. In the world, by and large, incredulity will be the rule rather than the exception. New continents will have been discovered by then which the Ancients had not even heard of by name. Numberless towers of Babel will dot the cities. Priests will grow hoarse preaching to the deaf. Parts of the human body will be interchangeable from one person to the other. The average temperature will rise, and drinking water shall be scarce. Men's sight and minds will focus on mere reflections of reality. And though John of

---

[2] For the information concerning this "Secret Protocol," we are indebted to Henri Perney, *Les miracles chrétiens, La prevue que Dieu existe* (Ed. Résiac, 5315 Montsûrs, 2018: pp. 43-46).

Jerusalem does not use the expression, society will turn into a "melting pot" of races. Women will be able to conceive beyond their appointed menopause. Children will be selected in the womb of their mothers from which those who are unwanted will be aborted. Many men, for lack of work, will remain idle.

"The sun will scorch the earth, the atmosphere will be a mere curtain with holes." "The sea will rise as boiling water and drown the coastal towns." Genetic manipulations of animals are foretold. Fiction will compete with fact in the transmission of information. Jews and Moslems will strife unceasingly in Palestine.

II. Astonishingly enough, John of Jerusalem locates in part two of his prophecies the conquest of the skies and of the deep blue sea. Feminism such as we know it is also foretold. Ultimately, there will be a spiritual renewal in conformity with the one which we describe in our book. In conclusion, John of Jerusalem read the future as if it were already history. He was one step ahead of St. Nilus.

Humanity did not stumble unknowingly into the era in which major sins are casually accomplished, and where even murder is permissible, as in the case of abortion or euthanasia. Can the unregenerate pursuit of evil ever be forgiven, "either in this world or the next"? And since nations, as earthbound entities, are not answerable in the hereafter for crimes committed in time and space, it is at the Endtimes that they will reap the consequences of the evil they committed. Just as the Deluge wiped out the generations responsible for an almost universal sinfulness in the days of Noah, a Judgment of Nations, a Parousia for collective responsibilities will conclude our two thousand years-old AD.

Some nations will be erased from the surface of the earth, flooded as was Atlantis for instance. Others will shrink, or, positively, will receive increase. Some provinces will be singled out for special treatment, because of exceptional crimes or, contrariwise, major accomplishments.

And since nations are of this world, it is in this very world that they will be judged according to their deserts and served with the "bowl of the fury of God." They may, at least, be partially spared in the name of worthy accomplishments, however. It is touching to see that God, for instance, singles France's province of Bretagne for milder treatment than the rest of the country because of its past Marian devotion and many missionary vocations.

An individual, on the other hand, is responsible for himself, and it is at his death that irrevocable choices are recognized for what they are. Such is the truth to be made manifest at the Last Judgment.

Meet in its measures are the designs of Providence that shall be soon written on earth and in the sky in eschatological terms, as announced in the Apocalypse of St. John! In the meantime, let us not underestimate the gift of prophecy, for such is the charism of the few for the benefit of the many.

Indeed, "the spirit of prophecy," according to Joseph de Maistre, "belongs to the nature of man and will forever remain active in the world. If I am asked what this spirit is, I will answer that never have there been major events in the world that have remained unannounced in one way or another."3

---

3 As quoted from the *Soirées de Saint Pétersbourg* in Claude d'Elendil's book: *De Nostradamus à Alois Irlmaier* (Poland, Domus, 2017, p. 10).

That is why St. Paul could elevate the charism of prophecy to that of second-highest spiritual endowment exercised for the good of the Church: first comes apostleship, and then comes the spirit of prophecy. Teachers are listed in the third place, much to the detriment of the high opinion intellectuals have of their own role. That is why I can call on I Cor 12, 28; Eph 4, 11-13 and Rom 12, 6-7, to revoke the arbitrary claims of modern theologians to pass cursory judgment on supernatural visions and wonders. Only too often in the past have they negated what was of God, in the name of abstract principles. Christ himself did not tolerate criticism from Pharisees who, as guardians of the Law, denied the workings of the Spirit. Expertise in a given field is not a key to competence in other areas. Usually, however, it is bishops who exercise the power of discernment. After Rome had pronounced itself on the authenticity of La Salette, Msgr. Genouilhac of Grenoble ruled on the credit that was to be given to the prophecies of Mélanie and Maximin, with the famous formula: "The role of the visionaries has ceased, the role of the Church begins." The trouble was that he thus obfuscated for more than a century the believability of the future foreseen by the two seers. Today, when this future has become reality, his restrictions have become redundant. And yet they have continued to be observed to this day.

For all practical purposes, however, the harsh critique of "cesspools of impurity" applied to churchmen by Mélanie meets with the approval of recent Popes after the scandal of pederast priests and dignitaries.[4]

---

4 That there would be a dramatic fall off in Faith and mores on the part of the Church body in apocalyptic times has always been common knowledge. In comparison, it should be worse on the part of the clergy.

"Such a gift of prophecy" has been relegated only too often to the background. It should come to the fore now that the times are ripe. God would not be God if his granting of such a charism spelled out the future for our benefit without appealing to our consciences. "Peter, do you love me?" was the question Christ addressed to the apostle who had denied him thrice. The doubt expressed by his master wounded Peter to the core. We who have not yet been confronted by the menace of arrest or execution for our following of Christ should not assume that circumstances will always be so favorable that we shall never be challenged. The Gospel has told us that a time would come when such a commitment will be as perilous as it had seemed to Saint Peter questioned by the servants of the Sanhedrin:

"You will be hated by all nations for my name's sake" (Mt 24, 9).

This universality of reprobation is the novelty that will confront us both in the "Endtimes" and at the End of Time, when "many will fall away, and will betray one another, and will hate one another." Denunciation will involve relatives, so that there will be no security in anonymity or solidarity to expect from any quarter, not even one's own family (Mt 24, 10). Blood ties will be of no avail:

"[For] brother will deliver up brother to death, and the father his child, and the children will rise against the parents and have them put to death; and you will be hated by all for my name's sake" (Mk 13, 12-13).

Just as the apostles disbanded at the arrest of Jesus, so will the body of the Church seemingly disintegrate at the coming of the Antichrist. Few will there be who, from lack of prayer and watchfulness, will not "enter under temptation" (Mk 14, 38).

This is what Pascal meant when he wrote that "the agony of Christ will last until the end of the world." He might have added for clarity, "and in the personhood of the Church as his Bride."

This quote is the clue to our forthcoming debate between the Endtimes and the End of Time as to the disasters to be assigned to the one or to the other.

What is confusing in the light of the previous evocation is that no clear distinction is made in the Gospel between what pertains properly to the one or to the other, all the more that a more immediate catastrophe was to be expected for the Jews with the destruction of their Temple.

"Our Lady of the Apocalypse" shall be of assistance, however, since she is appearing under different titles, the world over, to warn us of the seriousness of the hour and bringing, as a solicitous Mother, clarity to this debate on the future layers of forthcoming history.

"Now write... what is to take place hereafter" (Ap 1, 19).

I

THE COMING OF THE KINGDOM

"It would be mistaken to believe that our Lord would be satisfied with a reign in the sole privacy [of the individual heart of man]." (Father Dehon, Founder of the "Priests of the Sacred-Heart").

"Our Father who art in heaven
Hallowed be thy name;
Thy Kingdom come,
Thy will be done on earth as it is in heaven."

According to the French philosopher Simone Weil, the "Our Father" testifies to the fact that God is not of this world. Heaven is his abode. Likewise, his Kingdom is not of this world, but in Heaven. That is why to pray for the "Coming of the Kingdom of God," is to pray for the dissolution of this world, and for the end of time. Since the Kingdom is for man the absolute Good, the Kingdom cannot be "of this world."[5]

---

5 *La Connaissance Surnaturelle*, Gallimard, Paris, 1950, pp.262-263. It is true that my summary does not do justice to the speculative terms in which she expresses herself.

The absolute is for hereafter, and our earthbound humanity is too contingent for the establishment of a perfect society. Thus, when we recite the Our Father we petition God for the abolition of life on earth. What a paradox! The creature knows no better way of honoring its Creator than to aspire for the proximate extinction of its own species.

Most of us would find such an interpretation aberrant. When Christ said: "The Kingdom of God is in your midst," or "within you," he meant that it is present in the hearts of men of good will. We are all asked to "be... perfect as [our] heavenly Father is perfect." Such an assignment would be impossible in a metaphysical perspective. In moral terms, however, such a striving is the leaven of perfection. The grace of God is "in our midst" insofar as it is "within us." The grace of God achieves what is impossible to man.

I suspect that many people, nonetheless, when they recite the Lord's Prayer, have the impression that they are praying for their coming in a Heaven hereafter. Do they realize, however, that this would imply the concomitant destruction of our world? Are the theologians who deny the possibility of an establishment of the Kingdom of God on earth for the "thousand years" assigned to it by the Apocalypse, aware that they are thereby excluding the literal interpretation of two demands of the "Our Father"?

Is there anybody in his right mind who would say: "Please Lord, we beg of you, do destroy this world which is unworthy of your divine concern"?

Nobody would be caught expressing himself in this fashion. We all wish in our utmost hearts for some kind of moral, social and religious evolution or reformation which would make of this world a more livable, more likable, and especially more loving place. Yet, what is a world in which everyone loves his neighbor? Is it not that very society which Christ preached and enjoined us to work for, and especially to pray for? - Yes, the Our Father in its first half is an eschatological prayer and we should read it in precisely those terms. The Coming of the Kingdom it evokes is good news, not only for the hereafter. Furthermore, it is a proximate reality, if not an immediate one.

Just as the Jews of pre-Christian antiquity were longing for the day when the Messiah would set all things right, we Christians aspire for the 1000 years during which Christ will reign. "Is it now that you will reestablish the Kingdom of Israel" asked the apostles to Christ just before he left them to return to his Father. His answer was not that their question was inappropriate in itself, but only in its timing. "It does not belong to you to know what are the times and the moments that the Father has established in virtue of his Sovereign Power" (Acts 1, 6-7). In other words, it is in the Father's hands that the Kingdom come on earth, not in yours. What is supernatural, cannot be achieved by human devices: it is a miraculous state of affairs, a promise of God's bounty. It will come at the right moment. You should petition for its coming with faith, perseverance and a joyful heart: "Almighty God, 'may thy kingdom come'."

This Kingdom is the purpose of Creation. It should have happened earlier. Original sin delayed its coming but did not preclude it forever.

The "when" of this Coming of the Kingdom is a mystery, we have been told. And the "how" of its Coming is no less a mystery. It is even a greater one, considering all the hedging which has taken place on the theological level in recent times. For we have been told very clearly that the Coming of the Kingdom does not imply a return of Christ distinct and separate from his Coming in glory for the Final Judgment. Articles 672, 676 and 677 of the *Catechism of the Catholic Church* are very explicit - so much so that they are always invoked as a refutation of the thesis I am exposing here. Who

3

am I then to stand up and contest the decision of the teaching Church? Let me reassure my listeners that such is not my intention. For the Catechism is not the only expression of the teaching Church today; and the ideas I am defending here are not my own, but those of the early Church Fathers, countless Saints and Mystics throughout the centuries, and, lo and behold, even those of 20th century Popes. If that is the case, you will ask, why have the faithful been left in the dark?[6]

Let me say at this point what has been my personal experience on this subject. I heard a friend of mine give a lecture on eschatology. I asked him afterwards why he had not mentioned, at least as a plausible hypothesis, the theory which I am upholding here. He answered that as a priest he felt bound, for prudential reasons, not to counter current opinion. "You, however, as a layman are free to do so, as long as you state that you wish to remain a true son of the Church and abstain from hazardous formulations."

Thus fortified by this reassurance, let me proceed with my exposition. For there is a question we must tackle.

First hypothesis: the Kingdom of God is on its way. After all, this is what the apostles expected.

Collateral question: Are we then to wait for a Kingdom without a King? Is Christ to reign *in absentia*?

Given the passage in Acts 1, 6-7 mentioned previously, we know that "the Kingdom of Israel will be reestablished." Now Israel, in the perspective of the Old Testament, is tied to God through some providential equivalent of the sacrament of marriage. God has wooed her and won her as his Bride.

---

6 Let me assure my readers that the articles of the Catechism in question are not as explicit on this point as may be assumed from their hasty reading. For more details on this problem, see chapter 43 "De magisterio ordinario" of my book: *Is Mary appearing today?* (Goodbooks media, Corpus Christi, 2018).

When Israel, however, broke the bond by betraying her vocation and killing the Messiah, it is the resurrected Christ who became the mystical spouse of the new Israel, his own Church. As it was with the Bridegroom, however, so will it be with the Bride. She too will suffer betrayal, passion and death, even though the "Gates of Hell" will not ultimately prevail against her. She will recover from her apparent demise through an easterly resurrection of her own while her enemies are overcome. Will she then benefit from visitations of her Spouse as the apostles did of the apparitions of Christ during the forty days after Easter, and what is the "way" in which Christ will return, as the angels said he would do at the Ascension?

"This Jesus, who was taken up from you into heaven, will come in the *same way* as you saw him go into heaven" (Acts 1, 11).

Or, according to a more literal translation:

"This same Jesus, which is taken up from you into heaven, shall so come in like manner as ye have seen him go into heaven."[7]

Let us mention that the departure of Christ, in the presence of the eleven apostles, was as discreet as possible. It was as far removed as it could be from Elijah's own triumphal ascent in the presence of Elisha. For "behold, a chariot of fire and horses separated the two of them. And Elijah went by a whirlwind into heaven" (2 Kings, 2, 11).

If Christ returns for his Second Coming as unobtrusively as when he left, then it must have more in common with his First Coming, than with his Third Coming ("in the Glory of

---

7 The first translation is that of the Revised Standard Version of the Bible (Oxford University Press, 2002); the second is from the King James Version, Standard Text Edition (Cambridge University Press).

the Father"). Yet, as a curtain raiser for this unassuming return, there will be a conflagration of elements second to none, except for that which will take place at the world's end. We have here an analogical interplay of a most intriguing character. Nature was quiet on Christmas night and Christ was greeted by a pastoral rejoicing of shepherds. But for the Second Coming, Nature will groan and lament as a woman in labor. There will be ominous signs in heaven while men quake with fear: the sun will darken and the moon will turn red and the waters on earth will take on the color of blood. And the mystics say that the Cross will appear in the sky for all to see.

Thus, Christ will return to reign, after being heralded by a cosmic upheaval. But how will he reign?

Joseph Iannuzzi thinks Christ will reign through his invisible presence in the Eucharist.[8] What a contrast with the preceding catastrophes! As with Elijah, God is not in the storm, but in the soft wind. "Learn from me that I am humble and meek of heart." After the unrepentant major part of humanity has been wiped out by a fall of stars, an era of gentle spiritual intercourse will set in. The cloistered silence of prayer will settle as a dew on mankind. Furthermore the peaceful coexistence of lion and lamb will express this harmony, as if nature at last shared the benefits of redemption.

It is not I who say this, but the prophet Isaiah. Could he have been mistaken? Was he speaking merely in metaphors? It is a solace indeed to find in the Old Testament a reassuring counterpoint to the disastrous stridency of the New Testament prophecies ushering in our last and

---

8 In *The Triumph of God's Kingdom in the Millennium and End Times* (St. John the Evangelist Press, Havertown, PA, 1999, p.117).

6

momentous millennium.

If an era of peace is to set in, let it be that which allows for adoration and thanksgiving. The paradox, however, lies in the contrast between what was before and what comes after. For there has been no shortage of heroic virtue on an individual level throughout the two thousand years of Christendom. What this practice of the precepts of the Gospel lacked was a collective dimension. In the Middle Ages, for instance, when in Europe all men were united in a commonality of belief, they were divided nonetheless by what seemed a conflict-ridden pagan-like heritage of violent behavior. Once lost at the time of the Reformation, the unity of faith no longer constituted a ministering bond of peace. At war within itself, Christianity lost its hold on society, decidedly secularized in modern times. What the new world born out of the destruction of the old world will promote is not only the Kingdom of God **within** each one of us, but **in the midst** of us through the supernatural tie of charity. Thus the purpose of Christ's mission will have been fulfilled after a dismal picture of partial success, and subsequent failure, or at least apparent failure.

We are now dealing with the period following what Marie des Vallées called "the deluge of fire."9 On this burned-up planet recovering from the destruction of Babylon, a civilization of love will flourish. Christ will be our King, invisibly enshrined in the Eucharist, according to Father Iannuzzi.

Let us admit this as plausible of an answer as we can hope for to the question of the nature of Christ's presence. It has the advantage that it skirts all theological objections. The

9 Marie des Vallées was a 17th century mystic and victim soul: a friend of St. Jean Eudes who promoted the devotion to the hearts of Jesus and Mary.

way in which Christ will exercise his power, however, in this Kingdom of his, remains to be described. We know it should be unhindered, since Satan and his minions will have been locked in hell. Furthermore, there is no shortage of available documentation on the nature of the Kingdom of God. In fact, there is so much information available on this topic in the Bible that it is more than I can handle in this short book.

In order to proceed, let us return to the theme with which we were dealing: the three first requests of the Our Father. They are so intimately related to one another that they should be considered as a whole.

"Hallowed be thy name" means that we are praising God for his divine attributes, and above all for his goodness, mercy and providence. Such is the central point of our worship: it is our way of preparing ourselves on earth for the part we will play in the heavenly liturgy of paradise.

As for the "Thy kingdom come," it is not self-explanatory, for its meaning is clarified by the request that follows: "May Thy will be done on earth as it is in Heaven." Indeed, nothing is more worthwhile than the accomplishment of God's will. Since God is Love, his Will is that we should love as we are loved, and love each other as we cannot help but love ourselves. A reign of love should be Heaven on Earth. Is this an impossibility? Considering the present state of affairs on our planet, it certainly sounds like Utopia. How often have men dreamt of a society in which everyone would collaborate for the good of all! However, the second request - "May thy Kingdom come" should bear on a state of affairs which would be eminently desirable for *hic et nunc*. Is this metaphysically and theologically possible? For we are not expected to petition Heaven for something that is totally implausible. Our *lex orandi* serves as a blueprint for our *lex credendi*.

Israel as it Should Be

Luther thought that the precept of perfection embodied in the scriptural precept "Be ye perfect as your Heavenly Father is perfect" was the expression of a deplorable sense of humor on the part of divinity. God was asking us to reach for something unattainable. It is not so remote, however, an accomplishment as to be merely impossible. For if the total lack of sinfulness which it implies is restricted to the Virgin Mary, its realization is nonetheless one that, in spite of human weakness, is fulfilled in the apostle's word: "It is no longer I who live, but Christ who lives in me." What is feasible here individually with God's grace on the part of a mystic should be feasible collectively when Heaven grants a favorable answer to the second and the third request of the Lord's Prayer.

This is not merely a hypothesis: it is a prophecy. We find it expressed as early as in the Old Testament. It represents for our world the most optimistic part of the message of Revelation. It describes so enchanting a future as to have cradled in hope the undying faith of Israel. That the Jews in the time of Jesus misunderstood the promises made in the past by interpreting them in materialistic terms is the dramatic illusion which haunts their descendants to this day. Nonetheless the present return of Israel in the Land of its ancestors is what brings the happiness pledged by God for his people closer to fulfillment. This is at least what St. Paul tells us:

"And Jerusalem will be trodden down by the Gentiles, until the times of the nations be fulfilled.. . . . .
Even so, when you see these things coming to pass, know that the Kingdom of God is at hand" (Lk 21, 24 & 31).

Do we have to explain? The fact that Jerusalem is no longer "'trodden down by the Gentiles," means that "the

9

times of the nations" are "fulfilled." But what is the nature of this fulfillment? It means that a period of time has been completed, or more precisely a period of "times', for this plural signifies two thousand years, the two millenaries from Christ to our own days during which the nations have offered a distorted version of what the Kingdom of God should be. To the **times** of this corruption of a messianic ideal succeeds the **time** of the Kingdom, that very millennium announced in the Apocalypse.

That modern Israel is in biblical terms an aberration does not preclude the possibility that this very Zionism which led to the creation of a nation-state has providential implications. It announces far more than what it has attained. The Jews, in their pursuit of an earthly kingdom, have fulfilled the prophecy concerning the proximate coming of the Kingdom of God, even though the latter is not to be confused with the former. "These things [having come] to pass, [we should] know that the Kingdom of God is at hand."

For every accomplishment of a heavenly design, there are manifest signs, such as the one mentioned above, but there are also indications of a more spiritual nature. God arouses prophets. Not all are as spectacular as St. John the Baptist, the Precursor of Christ. Not yet, at least. For in our days, prophets are as discreet as were sister Faustina or Luisa Piccarreta. The first one with her posthumous message of God's mercy, the second one with the delayed publication of her notebooks on "the true Reign of the Divine Will on Earth." Specifically, Luisa was foretelling "The Fulfillment of the Our Father's third request: "may Your will be done on earth as it is in Heaven" ("Fiat voluntas tua, sicut in coelo et in terra"). .

This mystic, who lived at Corrato in Puglia, Southern Italy (1859-1947), was chosen by the Lord as a victim-soul to announce the coming of a new spirituality. As all valid novelties, however, the spirit of obedience to God it describes is as old as Christianity, since it is the one which the Blessed Virgin exercised perfectly. According to the expression of Bernanos it is even "older than sin": it goes back to the time before the Fall when Adam and Eve lived in a state of innocence. Without in the least implying that those, who would practice it as Luisa Piccarreta did, could partake of Mary's privilege of Immaculate Conception, it did signify that they could reach a state of sanctity unheard of until then. Luisa was to be the first of many who, under the guidance of the Holy Spirit, would pronounce a "fiat," consecrating themselves to the accomplishment of God's will by surrendering totally their own will to his. This would mean that, according to the Apostle's word: "It is not I who live, but Christ who lives in me." Among such forerunners of a world which seems more of Heaven than of earth, let us mention not only Luisa, but also Sister Faustina.

On earth, the greatest sacrifice of all is the surrender of one's freedom, not by its denial, but by its total commitment. The capacity of a faculty is measured by its object. And since there is no greater consecration than that which a saint makes of his will to God, he thereby fulfills the purpose he was created for. A parable of sorts will illustrate this point:

I happen to be driving my car, in which by the very privilege of my Baptism, Christ has taken place. As long as I am in a state of grace, he sits by my side. If I do not ask him, I go wherever I feel like. If I ask him, he tells me where to go, and I do so. If I ask him often enough which is the best road to follow, and show my immediate willingness to do what he says, I am on the road to perfection. The surest way, however, of staying on this path of righteousness, is to ask to my divine copilot: "Please, won't you drive instead," and exchange seats with Him. Then, God is in charge one hundred per cent, and His will alone is the way I am following. Is He not "the way, the truth and the life"? In his relation to His Father, Christ did not strive for autonomy. He was obedient unto death: "Not my will, but Thy will be done!"

There is another parable, which (like the previous one) I owe to Johannes de Parvulis, and which helps to illustrate this point:

Let us imagine a game of chess where the black checkers always seem to win. Upon closer observation, the reason for this is that the blacks follow a strategy, while the whites do not seem to do so. This is strange indeed, for the blacks are moved by the devil, while the whites are moved by God. However, as Napoleon once said: "victory depends for 90 % on execution, and only 10 % on strategy." The minions of Satan have surrendered to their master's will, that is why they carry it out so exactly: they march as automatons to his every beck and call. Satan's tool of subversion is the determinism that the surrender to their passions inflicts upon the unregenerate. Among the white checkers, Christ's gift is the spirit of freedom. The blacks are held in thrall by fear. The whites are inspired by love, and love is not compulsive. Thus, only too often, do these white checkers act on their own, instead of hearkening to God's instructions. Not seldom, divine strategy, thus hampered by private initiative, is thwarted, while, in contrast, devilish purpose is carried out relentlessly. But if success can crown temporal achievements, it cannot determine the ultimate future, which remains in God's hands.[10]

Thus, whatever victory is Satan's today, it will not cancel

---

10   The devil, furthermore, enjoys from the start a tactical advantage, which is that his purpose is the destruction of the City of God, which the followers of Christ are patiently constructing. Which is the easier task?

that of God tomorrow. In a message to a little soul, Christ expressed himself as follows:

"The modern world renews my Passion! However if all my Priests left me, as my Disciples did at my crucifixion on Golgotha, even if I remained alone with only one of them, as I remained alone with John, even so, through this one I will renew the world!"[11]

Thus the modern Church will be reduced to the very few. "When the Son of Man returns, will he still find faith on earth" (Lk 18, 8)? Objective observation of the loss of faith among Catholics, either through their explicit rejection of belief, or their selective dissent, should lead us to conclude that the return of Christ is at hand.

---

11   As quoted by Johannes de Parvulis in *Les Temps à venir* (Parvis, Hauteville, Switzerland, 2003, p. 180).

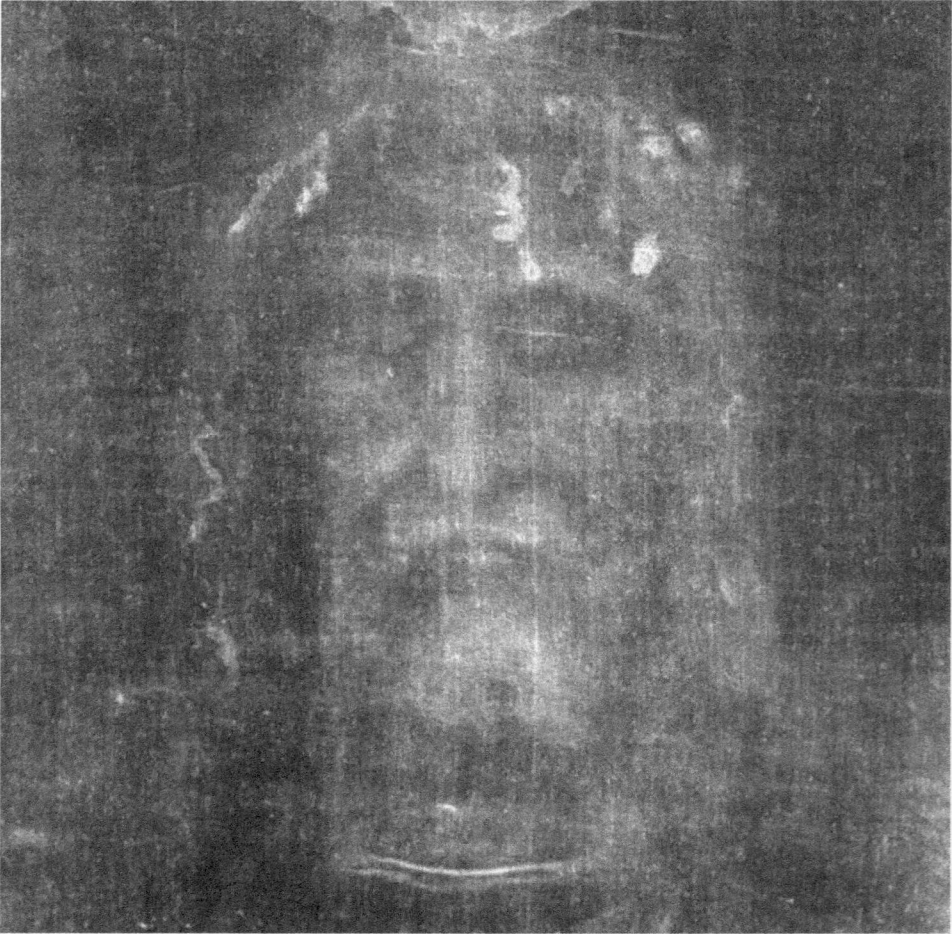

The Shroud of Turin

II

THE KINGSHIP OF JESUS

His claim to Kingship is a well-established fact.
    "All things were made through Him,
        and without Him was made
        nothing that has been made.
    He was in the world,
        and the world was made through Him...
    He came unto his own..." (Jn 1, 3, 10-11)

Furthermore, the words of the Our Father alone are a convincing enough argument in favor of our thesis that there will be a Kingdom of God on earth before there is one for all the elect in Heaven. Or at least there should be one, because God does not want us to pray for what is unattainable.

The very angel of the Annunciation testifies to the accomplishment of this prophecy:

"[Thy] son...shall be great and shall be called the Son of the Highest: and the Lord God shall give unto him the throne of his father David:

And he shall rule over the house of Jacob forever, and of his Kingdom there shall

be no end" (Luke I, 32-33).

Let us not make the mistake to think that these words are not to be taken literally.

15

Readers of the Gospel only too often tend to dismiss this interpretation on the grounds that Christ himself declined the title of King which his followers would have liked to give Him. He did not wish to be taken then as the glorious Messiah, but as the suffering Messiah, the man of sorrow in whose mouth Isaiah placed the words: "Sum vermis et non homo."

The only time when he welcomed the title was when, entering Jerusalem on an ass, five days before his Passion, the crowd greeted him with the words: "Blessed be the King that cometh in the name of the Lord..." "Blessed be the Kingdom of our father David, that cometh in the name of the Lord" (Luke 19, 38, Mc 11, 10). He even rebuked the Pharisees who found fault with these titles: "I tell you that, if these should hold their peace, the stones would cry out."

Furthermore, the clinching argument which swayed Pilate into condemning Jesus to death was that "whosoever maketh himself a king speaketh against Caesar" (Jn 19, 12). To claim such a title was provocation enough for the Proconsul, just as, hours before, Jesus' admission to the Sanhedrin that He was the Son of God had been the damning evidence against Him (Lk 22, 70).

Thus Jesus died for stating that he was both King and God.[12]

Just as he would to prove his divinity to his apostles through his Resurrection, he will come to his own as our King when he returns on the clouds of heaven over two thousand years later.

---

12 He was born a king and he would die because of his rightful claim to this title. Jewish rabbis to this day are aware of the contrast in the prophecies between the suffering Messiah and the glorious Messiah. As a result they supposed there would be two Messiahs. Alas, most of them will, at first, take the Antichrist for their long-awaited Savior.

"...and of his kingdom there shall be no end" writes Luke. This is the very kingdom which, after a flourishing "thousand years" on earth, will seemingly be overrun briefly by Gog and Magog, i.e. Satan and his earthly accomplices. Yet it will be reinstated in a transfigured form in Heaven after the Final Judgment.

Let us not minimize the attribution of an earthly Kingship to Jesus, as if that of the Son of God did not suffice. The first title is due to Him as man, the second one because of his divinity. Christ was of royal lineage, that of David, and when he came to Israel, he came unto his own. Yet He was rejected by his own for claiming to be more than a man, just as he was put to death by the Roman rulers on the suspicion of fostering national aspirations. He could have been accepted by the Jews as their Messiah, if he had not insisted on being accepted as God. In the same way, he would have been exonerated by Pontius Pilate, had he not been accused by the Sanhedrin of that which had been but a minimal claim on his part. Thus both dignities were refused to He who was born both of God and of David.

Only too often do Christians who readily worship Christ as God omit to give him his due as King. The image on the Holy Shroud testifies that he was of kingly stature, his features were those of a Monarch. We can say he looked the part, with his 1, 95 meter, when the average height of men was 1,60-1,70 m, and, as the Bible prophesied: "the most handsome of the sons of men."[13]

---

13 How do we know that Christ was so tall? Most scholars think he was 1 m, 80 on the basis of the measurements of His imprint on the Holy Shroud of Turin. But as François Giraud points out, they neglect to take into account the *rigor mortis* which froze the body in the position it had on the Cross. The neck and the knees were bent forwards, the Crown of Thorns preventing the head from resting on the wood, and the burden of

To be precise, he reminds us in his portrait on the Holy Shroud of the Kings of Assyria as they were portrayed in stone: and this is no doubt a genetic legacy of the Babylonian captivity on the part of his ancestors.

These are not incidental details. His eloquence was such that, since the Gospel is in circulation, writers have tried to match, without really succeeding, in spite of the handicap that Christ can only be read in translation.[14]

"O my Lord and my God," such is our traditional address. Thus we mention his human sovereignty first, and rightly so, since He became flesh so as to be one of us.

Let us be consistent: just as Christ's true nature is now part of our creed, so should his sovereignty be part of our worship.

There is another claim of Jesus to his Kingship which is often overlooked and which was as crucial in his condemnation as those grounds on which he officially deserved to be crucified which we have mentioned above: this is his affirmation that he rules a Kingdom which is not of this world. He was answering the query: "What hast thou done?" (Jn 18, 36). Once again it is by right of birth that he rules. To the question "Art thou a king then?" he responds:

"Thou sayest that I am a king. To this end was I born, and for this cause came I into the world, that I should bear

---

the body weighing on the legs. (See *Etudes et Révélations sur le Linceul*, Editions Rassemblement à son Image, Plouisy, 2017, pp. 273-302).

14   Strangely, it is Nietzsche, the promoter of the "death of God" theory, who perhaps tried most to match his style in terms of pungency. Paradoxically, he succeeded when he formulated what was and remains the gist of the matter: "God is dead. And it is we who have killed Him." We, men of those times who plotted against him, or we today, when we banish him from our hearts or uproot his teaching from our culture.

witness unto the truth. Everyone that is of the truth heareth my voice."

Pilate's reaction is well-known: "What is truth?" as if he were speaking to himself because he does not expect a reply. The debate is not about truth, that very truth which testifies of the innocence of Jesus, but of what is expedient.

These three words were Our Lord's undoing. That is why he suffered "under Pontius Pilatus." Skepticism is indifference to value: it is subjectivism at its worst, that which addresses the sphere of morality. Nothing is absolute because private interest and personal advantage are ultimately the last resort in decision making for a careerist. Jesus' death could be said to be a casualty of pragmatism.

At the same time, it is paradigmatic. Pontius Pilatus was questioning the objectivity of truth: he would have many followers, from then on, until modern philosophy seemingly took its cue from him.

The denial of the Kingship of Jesus can be said to be the "sin against the Holy Ghost," the touchstone of evil in recurrent times up to today, as the following story will illustrate.

In the first part of the twentieth century, there was in Paris an humble nun called Sister Olive Danzé who bore the stigmata of Christ. She had been told that, just as a basilica had been built to honor the Sacred Heart, the Lord wished that the same be done in recognition of his Kingship[15]. The unbelievable happened: Sister Olive promoted the heavenly project, had leaflets printed, begged for contributions, and against all human expectations, succeeded in raising the necessary funds: an imposing sanctuary on the grounds of her order (1932-1956) dedicated to "Christ the King." Hardly

---

15   By then Pope Pius XI had already instituted the Feast of Christ the King (1926).

had it been built that a campaign, initiated by some narrow-minded members of her own congregation, brought about her disgrace: Sister Olive was banished to Brittany where she remained in seclusion until her death. Eventually, some real-estate promoters convinced the archbishop of Paris, cardinal Marty, that the overall decline of Church-attendance justified the sale of the newly erected church. The few sisters left were relocated elsewhere while their convent and adjacent church were torn down in 1977, to be replaced by apartment buildings. What Cardinal Marty did not know - or if he knew, neglected to take into account - was that our Lord had warned Sister Olive that with the destruction of this sanctuary, the town of Paris would lose the last shield protecting it from its own imminent ruin. Since the prophecies of La Salette, and many others, we Frenchmen are aware that our capital shall suffer one day the fate foretold to Babylon. A suspended sentence hangs above it.

Paris is targeted for oblivion, for it is - though not exclusively - the emblematic whore whom St. John describes as the "woman... arrayed in purple and scarlet, decked with gold and precious stones and pearls, holding a golden cup in her hand full of the abominations and filthiness of her fornication..." "Drunken with the blood of the martyrs of Jesus... [she sits] upon the scarlet beast who is full of names of blasphemy and has seven heads and ten horns" (Apoc 17, 1-4). Was Paris not the first Christian capital to abolish religion and to export revolution abroad? Was it not then at the heart of that very Free Masonry whom the Apocalypse describes as "the great dragon, having seven heads and ten horns, and seven crowns upon his heads" who threatens that other Woman who stands for the Church (12, 3)?

Thus Christ, through his mystics and his saints, keeps proposing supernatural solutions to problems arising from our sins, while Churchmen keep brushing them aside. How long did it take for Mary's request at Fatima to the Pope to be fulfilled? And how great was the success once it was implemented! The wall dividing Europe fell. A simple act of consecration had changed the course of history. Can it do so forever, however? Many other requests have been made recently by visionaries in the name of Mary, and these - sad to say - have fallen upon deaf ears. Instead of listening to what the Virgin says, Churchmen only too often quibble about the authenticity of apparitions and of messages from Heaven. When at San Damiano pilgrims answer the call of Mary, the bishop of Piacenzia writes to all the bishops of Europe to forbid their faithful from coming. When at Medjugorje fallen-away Christians convert daily by the dozens or the hundreds, the local bishop neglects to invite John-Paul II who would have wished to celebrate a Mass there. The pretext is often that the apparitions might be diabolical... as if "Beelzebul would chase Beelzebul."

The downfall of the Church, announced at La Salette, will be caused by its widespread suspicion of what seems too supernatural to be true.

But if the demise of the Church is imminent, what of its resurrection?

What will be the state of things before the "end of times"?

Just as Moses, Kings and Prophets have announced the First Coming of Christ, so have prophets, mystics and saints foretold his Return, and his resulting Reign.

One oft-neglected episode of Joan of Arc's life illustrates this point. This seventeen-year old Maiden was commissioned by Heaven to crown as King of France the legitimate heir, the Dauphin. When she arrived at his court of exile at Chinon in 1529, she told this reluctant Prince that God required of him that he officially declare and recognize Christ as the true Sovereign of the French nation, such as it had been proclaimed by St. Remi with the assent of King Clovis in the VIth century. The Dauphin realized that since he had nothing to lose, an official document was established to that effect, duly notarized and placed on the altar of the local Church. This preliminary step accomplished, Joan could take over the leadership of the French army and lead it from victory to victory until Charles was crowned at Rheims. It was at least implicitly assumed that he was henceforth the vicar of the Heavenly Monarch. Such symbolic gestures attest that Christ claims a more than figurative lordship over countries, as he does over individuals.

Louis XIV was expected by Heaven, according to its messenger Marguerite Marie Alacoque, to confirm Christ's claim to leadership by placing the effigy of the Sacred Heart on the flags of the French army. Victory would be his if he did so. This worldly Monarch did not give credence to a nun's request. Was it as a long delayed requital of this refusal that his heir, Louis XVI, a century later, would lose both throne and life? This unfortunate monarch, once imprisoned, thought that such had been the case.

These are too many steps on the way which point to the future Great French Monarch, of Bourbon lineage, foretold as the herald and effective ruler of both a Christianized Europe and a peaceful Middle East, under the sovereign tutelage of God to be ignored!

This forthcoming event has been announced by innumerable voices of mystics and prophets, such as those of St. Francis of Paule (1469), Mélanie Calvat of La Salette (1854), Marie-July Jahenny (1877-1922), and the visionary of Kérizinen (1938-1965).

Such as the future will be, it will be implementing what had already been foretold in broad strokes in the Old Testament, from the very first Psalms, both of Christ as God and as King:

"The Lord hath said unto me. Thou art my Son, this day I have begotten thee.

Ask of me, and I shall give thee the heathen for thine inheritance, and the uttermost parts of the earth for thy possession."

And how shall this come to be?

"Thou shalt break them with a rod of iron: thou shalt dash them in pieces like a potter's vessel" (Psalm 2).

This second part of this program shall be an exercise of might upon a fraudulent sovereign, one no less than the Prince of Evil and of the Legions of Hell on earth.[16]

---

16 For details on this second part, see our chapter 11, sections 10-12.

**A vision of hell on earth
according to Hieronymus Bosch**

III

SATAN, THE PRINCE OF THIS WORLD

Whether we like it or not, the Devil is entitled to this title.

Not as legitimate ruler, no doubt, but as an upstart potentate.

He claims ownership of the world, thus "bearing witness to himself," which is legally not valid. Yet this claim reflects dismal reality.

Though this rule of Satan is morally questionable, it is a fact of which he can boast and he does so in no uncertain terms when he tempts Jesus in the desert.

That Satan rules is even to a degree a fact of our own lives.

We live in the world he has fashioned to suit his fancy, as a projection of himself, which we share whenever we place ourselves, through mortal sin, under his active tutelage.

The proof of what I say is to be found in Biblical texts and is confirmed by observation.

We are loathe to recognize this, but the world of today is very much the devil's making, just as it is Eve's legacy.

Death, sickness, and the triple concupiscence of the eyes, of the flesh and of this world, are the universal consequence of sin; and let us not forget the penalty of war as Cain's own contribution.

The very animals share the burden of an existence which is ours by right since we asked for it, and under which yoke they pine, without having any responsibility or any say in the matter.

Were it only for them, we humans who are tender-hearted and moved to tears by their unnecessary suffering, should be ashamed of our responsibility in their present plight. They who had lived in Paradise from the vegetation of the trees and of the grass of the earth are now mainly cannibalizing each other, so to speak, as they prey on one another, from one higher species to a lower one.

"And God said, 'Behold, I have given you every plant yielding seed which is upon the face of all of the earth, and every tree with seed in its fruit; you shall have them for food. And to every beast of the earth, and to every bird of the air, and to everything that creeps on the earth, everything that has the breath of life, I have given every green plant for food" (Gn 1, 29-30).

The very elements are out of kilter now, however, as if the world were trying to challenge our right to be there. Its maladjustment is also our doing, even though the initiative comes from the Devil.

Why seek in geological rifts the cause of earthquakes, volcanoes and tsunamis, when their dynamic impetus results from our past or present association "with principalities, powers, world rulers of this present darkness and spiritual hosts of wickedness in the heavenly places" (Eph. 6, 12)?

These denizens of the outer spheres had enjoyed peace in the empyrean, until their leader, once his pride turned him into "a great red dragon, with seven heads and ten horns, and seven diadems on his heads" did sweep them "down on earth with his tail." Thus were "a third of the stars in heaven cast" down upon the earth" (Apoc 12, 3-4). In other words, a third of the angels, who were born as stars reflecting God's light.

Thus projected into the lower spheres in which we live and breathe, Satan and his minions brought with them a spirit of revolt which they communicated to our first parents.

Now sin has more power than all natural causes, and if it did not destroy the whole world, as a result, it is because God had placed a limit upon what is by its very nature limitless. Sin indeed is a proposition of independence from a Creator whose concern remains our own and only real good.

Thus, we men are only in part delivered unto the power of the Prince we have chosen as leader at a time of momentary madness. That is why we can oppose resistance to him if we wish and are able to cultivate our inner garden of virtue, the "Kingdom of God." It remains "within us" if we give it precedence over the "powers" that are at work in a society which they control by and large.

Had not St. Paul warned us that a time would come "when people will not endure sound teaching, but having itching ears they will accumulate for themselves teachers to suit their own fancies, and will turn away from listening to the truth to wander into myths" (2 Tim. 3-4)?

Paul Bouchard relates the preceding text, in which men are blinded by the fictions they foster when they renounce Christian Freedom, with the downfall of Satan:

"Woe to the inhabitants of the earth and of the sea! For the devil is come down unto [them], having great wrath, because he knoweth that he hath but a short time" (Apoc 12, 12).

Perversion has been placed today upon a pedestal for all to emulate, even though we are taken aback by it when it shows up in the criminal behavior of mere children. These juveniles fall prey to apparently unmotivated crime, with homicide practiced sometimes as a game. Diabolical possessions increase in number as they go unrecognized from clerical circles.[17]

St. Paul has announced what has become only too familiar to our generation:

"Thus know ye also, that in the last days, perilous times shall come" (2 Tim 3, 1). Why does evil peak and crest as an impending wave in this way on the waters of fleeting time? - The answer is that Satan reads prophecies more carefully than Churchmen do. As an aging potentate, as a Herod meeting out death sentences to his own sons before eliminating babies as potential rivals, Satan strikes wildly in despair: he knows his reign is coming to a close. He feels cornered by the apparitions of the Virgin: she will crush him with her foot. As the bearer of the light of the Enlightenment, at first, and then as the explosive instigator of revolutions, he has crowned with blasphemy the social constitution of nations. Now that his light is about to flicker out after its fiercest intensity, he preys on mankind with the energy of despair. Watch out humans, "quia leo rugit quaerens quem devoret" ("For the lion roars seeking whom to devour")!

Our next chapter should provide quite a contrast to the above situation: it deals with the world such as it should be with the grace of God. By then the constitution of the Kingdom of God will constitute for our benefit the very fabric of our social order.

As an additional reason to rejoice at the thought, let us consider the change for the better of our lower brethren, the animals. Could they too escape from their bondage to violence?[18]

---

17 Paul Bouchard, *Le règne de Dieu sur la terre* (Spirimédia, Chertsey, Québec, 1994, pp. 116-117).

18 On this topic, see chapter 8. If all things are to be renewed, should not animal behavior improve? This question is at the crux of the uncertainty which is ours. For the Reign of Christ will save us from a sinfulness comparable to the one which had been ours

for centuries. Satan has not achieved hell on earth, but he has created on the local level islands of perversion and of oppression that seem pretty close approximations of it.

Contrariwise, the Reign of Christ for a Millennium means a society of Saints, while taking into account the limitations of imperfection proper to all humans except for the Virgin Mary.

With animals, it is instinct which rules behavior: it should be difficult, therefore, to imagine a change radical enough to turn a lion into a sheep dog. For a nature more congenial to man, we must project into the future a process with has already taken place in the past: 150 million years ago, monsters roamed the earth. It seems unbelievable that men could have coexisted with them. Human footprints, however, have been found in sediments side by side with those of dinosaurs. With the exception of varans on an Indonesian island, these fearful creatures are extinct, no doubt as a result of the radical climatic change brought about by a large asteroid crashing on the peninsula of Yucatan. A kind of climatic deluge ensued. The impact sent up so many debris in the air that it triggered an ice-age fatal to most cold-blooded creatures. Hot-blooded ones appeared, almost as a result, to fill the gaps. A few could be domesticated: wolves evolved into dogs, tarpans into horses.

If dinosaurs have vanished following a natural disaster in the past, so could threatening species such as sharks in the sea or lions on the Veldt disappear as a consequence of that Great Tribulation programmed as a requital for the sinfulness of men...

This is speculation, but it is less far-fetched than children at play with cobras, or as Isaiah writes:
"The wolf and the lamb shall feed together,
The lion shall eat straw like the ox,
And dust shall be the serpent's food" (65, 25).

However nothing is impossible to God, and that is why we should not downplay arbitrarily the literal transcription of prophecies. A grey zone of uncertainty remains which we cannot impinge upon.

St. Michael fighting the Dragon, Albrecht Dürer

IV

THE EARLY CHURCH FATHERS

The message of the New Testament should be read through the eyes of those who were most likely to understand it correctly, the early Church Fathers. The earliest of these is **St. Papias** (70-150), to whom, according to St Irenaeus, John dictated his Gospel.[19] Papias describes a Kingdom, where "the just shall reign, after having resuscitated from the dead ...[while] creation... liberated and re-

---

19 See Iannuzzi, *La splendeur de la Création* (Leparex, 2008), p. 49-50. All the following quotations from the Church Fathers are taken from this book, chapter 3.1, pp. 47-78, even though Iannuzzi is by far not the only contemporary theologian to mention them and draw the same conclusions as I do here.

In the case of Pappias, if it is he who took dictation from St. John, his role as a confidant of the apostle might help explain Jn 21, 23: "This saying therefore went abroad among the brethren, that that disciple was not to die. But Jesus had not said to him, 'He is not to die'; but rather, 'If I wish him to remain until I come, what is it to thee?' This quotation can be taken as confirmation that the second generation of Christians was expecting a return of Christ in a not too distant future and, not implausibly, a prolongation of John's life for centuries to come.

newed, produces in abundance all kind of nourishment..."

As for **St. Justin**, martyr (100/110-165), he announces a time of universal peace.

"If you ever meet... Christians who do not accept this doctrine, do not consider them as true Christians... For I am certain,... that there will be a resurrection of the flesh followed by a thousand years in the town of Jerusalem, reconstructed, embellished and expanded, as foretold by Ezekiel, Isaiah and the other prophets."

St. Irenaeus of Lyon (140-202) sat at the feet of St. Polycarp of Smyrna (65-156), who in turn had known John the Apostle. We read the following in Iraeneus's book *Adversus Haereses*:

"After the Antechrist has reduced the whole world to a wasteland and reigned for three and a half years... the Lord will come on the clouds down from high heaven... and will send the Antechrist with his faithful into the lake of fire...

That is when the just will reign after being resurrected from the dead...

That is what the presbyters who have seen John, the disciple of the Lord, remember hearing him say, when he evoked the teaching of the Lord concerning these times...

Humanity will be in peace with itself, and so will Nature where crops will be bountiful and animals live in peace with each other."

The much quoted *Epistle of Barnaby* (130-131: author unknown) is informative. It establishes a correlation between the seven days of creation and the seven phases of humanity. These phases stretch over 7000 years, the last millennium being that of God's sabbatical rest, at which time God can relax. "His Son has brought to an end the times of injustice, judged the impious, metamorphosed the sun, the moon and the stars..." Nature has indeed been renewed, wedded as it is to the supernatural.

Tertullian (155-240), in his treatise *Contra Marcion*, announces that "an empire is to be ours on earth, an empire forerunner of Heaven, but in another state, arriving only after the Resurrection, and persisting for a thousand years in the Jerusalem descended from Heaven, that august city built by divine hands..." A true City of God foreshadowing its celestial counterpart.

More mundanely, **Saint Hippolytus** of Rome (170-235) shared this concept of the sabbatical rest of God that will introduce a time of peace on earth.

As for **Saint Methodius** of Olympia (+300), he calls the seventh millenary the "great day of the resurrection," in which sanctity shall prevail as never before.

The most explicit and eloquent Church Father is **Lactantius** (250-317). He reads the *Apocalypse* literally and announces a double defeat of evil: a temporary one at first, when the casting into hell of the false prophet, the Beast and all the devils introduces a millennium of peace; and secondly, an everlasting downfall, when after this interlude, the last-minute comeback of iniquity, in the guise of Gog and Magog, ushers in the Last Judgment.

"Consequently, the Son of God... will come... Once he has eradicated injustice and executed his great judgment and brought back to life the just... he will remain amongst men for a thousand years and will govern them with justice... The world itself will rejoice and nature will exult, liberated from the domination of evil, and of impiety, crime *and* error."

According to Joseph Iannuzzi, the expression "'Christ will remain amongst men for a thousand years' signifies essentially an interior and spiritual reign in the souls." The first judgment is executed over all unbelievers living at that time in the world: such is the first parousia. The second and final judgment, which takes place a thousand years later, concerns all of mankind.

Saint Cyril of Jerusalem (315-386), both Father and Doctor of the Church, makes a distinction between the first coming of Christ, when he is born of a Virgin, and "the second hidden coming as that of a rain on a fleece, and the third coming which takes place before the eyes of all..." The metaphor of "rain on a fleece" stands for the active intervention of the Holy Ghost whose era is that of the millennium.

Saint Augustine (354-430) was at first in this matter a follower of St. Iraeneus: "...this eighth day stands for the new life that will follow the end of centuries, just as the seventh designates the peaceful rest that the saints will enjoy on earth; because the Lord will reign there with his saints [...] Once the seven ages of this passing world will have ... gone by, we will return to this beatific immortality."[20]

Saint Bernard of Clairvaux (1090-1153) agrees: the second Coming of Christ is "invisible, while the two others are visible." This "intermediate Coming is hidden; the elect alone see the Lord in themselves, and they are saved." Discretion seems to be its distinctive feature.

As for **Saint Augustine**, his teaching on this theme is, to say the least, confusing. At first, in the *City of God* (chap 7) he describes the 1000 years mentioned in the Apocalypse as the sabbatical rest of the Saints "who will resuscitate to solemnize it." Then, in a further section of chapter 7, he equates the last millennium with the final state of perfection of souls. Lastly in the following chapter, he uses the 1000 years as a symbolic figure covering the state of the Church since the birth of Christ till the end of the world. Strangely enough, this last interpretation alone has been deemed wor-

---

[20] Saint Augustin, *Sermon 259*, as quoted by Françoise Breynaert (*Explications des Révélations de Maria Valtorta sur La Fin des Temps*, Rassemblement à son Image, Plouisy, 2018, p. 40).

thy of consideration by most of the theologians of the Middle Ages up to our days. They seemed to think that this last version had implicitly canceled the two previous ones.

More probably, Augustine was merely proposing tentatively a hypothesis for the benefit of whoever did not agree with tradition.

Thanks to God, **St. Bonaventure**, was of a different opinion. Thus it is noteworthy that cardinal Ratzinger, who wrote his PhD thesis on this Saint, mentions that Augustine's first version "has never been officially rejected or condemned by the Church." And this is good news, since it is precisely the glad tidings brought to us by the *Apocalypse*:

"Those who refused to worship the Beast and its image, and did not accept his mark upon their foreheads or upon their hands: they came back to life and reigned with Christ for a thousand years... This is the first resurrection" (Apoc 20, 4-6)."

That is why St. Bonaventure could write about "a time of peace at the times of the end.

Indeed, when after the great ruin of the Church, the Antechrist will be destroyed by Michael, after this supreme tribulation of the Antechrist there will come, before the day of Judgment, a time of such peace and tranquility, that there has not been such one since the Creation of the world, and men will be found there with a holiness comparable with that at the time of the Apostles" (Hexaëmoron, 16th conference).[21]

As for Cardinal Jean Daniélou, in his *A History of Early Christian Doctrine* (pp. 377, 379), he is convinced that St. John means what he says. Indeed, there will be "an intermediary stage in which the resuscitated saints are still

---

21 As quoted by Paul Bouchard: *Le règne de Dieu sur la terre* (Spirimédia/Parvis, Switzerland, 1994, p. 134).

on earth and have not yet entered into their final stage, for this is one of the aspects of the mystery of the last days which has not yet been revealed."

Furthermore, this first return of Christ has a special meaning for the Jews, for whom it will be the Coming of the second chance. They had been called upon, through providential ordination, to greet the Messiah collectively with the cry of welcome uttered at Christ's entrance in Jerusalem on Palm Sunday: "Hosanna! Blessed is He who comes in the name of the Lord! Blessed is the reign of our Father David that is coming!" (Mc 11, 9-10). But while this public recognition was comparatively small in scope and did not have a lasting impact on the populace as a whole, the Jews shall have the possibility to make up two thousand years later that about which they had been remiss. Will they, at long last, "recognize the signs of the times"? If John the Baptist has been the herald of Christ, with mitigated results, Elijah should play the same role before the return of Christ, hopefully with more success. This is what Jesus Sirach evokes when he writes:

"How glorious you were, Elijah, in your glorious deeds... At the appointed time, it is written, you are destined to calm the wrath of God before it breaks out in fury, to turn the hearts of parents to their children, and to restore the tribes of Jacob, happy are those who will see you, happy are those who have gone to sleep in the Love of the Lord, for we also, we shall possess the true life." (48, 4-11). Thus **St. John Chrysostom** (347-407) could announce the return of Elijah:

"Scripture tells us there will be two advents of Christ: one is in the past, the other is to come. The prophets mentioned both." In both cases, Elijah is involved, but the first time only figuratively, in the guise of John the Baptist; and the second time, in person. Thus Christ could announce:

"Elijah will come and he will restore all things" (Mt. 17; 11). 'This means, adds Chrysostomos, that he will correct the unbelief of the Jews..." How will he do that? - "He will reconcile he heart of the father with his son, ...that is to say that he will reconcile the mind of the Jewish people, with the belief of their sons, *id est* of the Apostles."

St. John Chrysostomos thus sets the conversion of the Jews shortly before the first return of Christ. Elijah will be instrumental in this change of heart which will "calm the wrath of God [towards his people] before it breaks out in fury" against the whole world (Sirach 48, 10).[22]

---

22 It is as if the Shoah, this Passion of the Jewish people, had bonded them mystically with that of Christ for the very purpose of their future conversion. For the way in which "the wrath of God... breaks out in fury" against sinful mankind, see next chapter. It is thus clear, from the above quotations, that the "great tribulation" should take place closely afterwards (Mt 24, 21). As for the quotations of St John Chrysostomos, see the *Magnificat* issue of Dec. 2010, Betton (France), p.146.

"And I saw a beast coming out of the sea, having seven heads and ten horns, and upon its horns ten diadems…" (Apoc 13, 1), Albrecht Dürer

V

THE NEW TESTAMENT

The message conveyed by the early Church Fathers is not one that we can shrug off and easily dismiss. They shared the living tradition of the Church at a time when it was only one, two, or very few generations removed from the immediate eyewitnesses of our Lord: they are reliable interpreters of the New Testament. Alas, if we may be so bold, however, as to consider their teaching with objectivity, they seem to have been somewhat remiss in their task. Concentrating as they did on what was essential, the better to refute nascent heresies and wild speculations, they did not analyze methodically the texts they relied upon. They were so busy in their "defense" of Faith that they somewhat neglected its "illustration." In their own way, their shortcoming, if I may be so bold as to say, was the very one of the authors of the New Testament who were so much taken up by their mission of evangelization, that they recorded the deeds and sayings of our Lord with but scanty regard to chronology or contextual differentiation. Let me give as an example the fact that the prophecies concerning the destruction of Jerusalem and those concerning the end times are all lumped together. The reader is not given advance notice either that there are two "end times": of which the second one alone is a definite *terminus ad quem*. And the most at fault of all in this respect is St. John in his Apocalypse. His excuse at least, is that his models Daniel, Isaiah, Ezekiel *et alii* were hardly paradigmatic in this respect. We are reassured, however, by the warning of Christ: "He who has ears to hear, let him hear!" In other words, men of good will are called upon to understand what remains concealed to lesser spirits. Pearls are not to be fed to swine. The mystery of iniquity is such that it casts a cloud on the mind of the sons of perdition. If we are in the end times, it is probably just as well that those who are marked with the sign of the Beast are not aware that their end is near. Prophecies are for the benefit of the elect.

For the Jews, Christ had this to say as he was about to die: "Jerusalem, Jerusalem! Thou who killest the prophets... you shall not see me henceforth until you shall say; 'Blessed is he who comes in the name of the Lord!' (Mt. 23, 37-39). For they shall "see" him whose heart they have "pierced" (Zech 12:10). This will be after their collective conversion, of which we now know retroactively that it could only take place after two thousand years.[23] For first must come the events which Matthew describes in the following terms for the benefit of Christians:

"...you shall hear of wars and rumors of wars (and of revolutions, as Luke adds). Take care that you do not be alarmed, for these things must come to pass, but the end is not yet. For nation will rise against nation, and kingdom against kingdom; and there will be pestilences and famines and earthquakes in various places. But all these things are the beginnings of sorrows.

Then they will deliver you up to tribulation, and will put you to death; and you will be hated by all nations for my

---

23 I must recognize that this is not the opinion of the majority of exegetes for whom the Jews will only convert shortly before the end of the world, and this would mean "after three thousand years." Time will show!

name's sake. And then many will fall away, and will betray one another; and will hate one another. And many false prophets will arise, and will lead many astray. And because iniquity will abound, the charity of many will grow cold. But whoever perseveres to the end, he shall be saved. And this gospel of the kingdom shall be preached in the whole world, for a witness to all nations; and then will come the end (24, 6-14; see also Mk 13, 9-10).

For then there will be great tribulation, such as has not been from the beginning of the world until now, nor will be. And unless those days had been shortened, no living creature would have been saved. But for the sake of the elect those days will be shortened" (Mt 24; 21-22).

Thus life will go on, for we are not at the end of the world, and our time likens that of Noah.

"...as it was in the days of Noah, even so will be the coming of the Son of Man be. For as in the days before the flood, they were eating and drinking, marrying and giving in marriage, until the day when Noah entered the ark, and they did not understand until the flood came and swept them all away; even so will be the coming of the Son of Man be.

"Then two men will be in the field, one will be taken, and one will be left. Two women will be grinding at the millstone: one will be taken, and one will be left. Watch therefore..." (Mt 24, 37-42).

Concerning this mysterious last verse, Luke is even more emphatic: "I say to you, on that night there will be two on one bed: one will be taken, and the other will be left." For that Coming of the Son of Man, even couples will be separated (Lk 17,34).

This should be quite a fitting and astonishing conclusion. Such a sudden removal of one from the company of the other is the finishing touch on the recital of a whole array of disconcerting events, whatever their chronology. But we have been properly warned, for there is no end in sight to the wonders of all nature to which men will be exposed:

"...false christs and false prophets will arise, and will show great signs and wonders, so as to lead astray, if possible, even the elect. Behold, I have told it to you beforehand. If therefore they say to you, 'Behold, he is in the desert', do not go forth; 'Behold, he is in the inner chambers,' do not believe it. For as the lightning comes forth from the East and shines even to the West, so also will the coming of the Son of Man be. Wherever the body is, there will the vultures be gathered together." (Mt 24, 24-28).

To what foreseeable event could the last sentence be alluding when it evokes the gathering of vultures around a corpse? Msgr Aldo Gregori thinks this carrion is either the sinner whose soul the devils are gathering to take to hell, or a symbolic expression for the sad state of the Mystical Body, the Church, which the sects are assailing as so many harpies.

After this dismal picture, let us rejoice at the following news:

"But when these things begin to come to pass, look up, and lift up your heads, because your liberation is at hand" (Lk 21,28).

Some translations say "because your redemption is at hand," as if Christ were alluding to the end of the world. But the Bible of Jerusalem speaks of "your deliverance," which is more appropriate an expression in the context of the intermediary Coming of the Lord, and at the onset of His Reign.

The "liberation" which is "at hand" is that from sin, and from our bondage to those leaders through which Satan rules our world. Even though one cannot speak of a non-transmission of original sin from one generation to the next, yet sinfulness such as it is lived today will be no more. Men will delight in peace, and cast swords into plowshares, while women will shun with horror the abortion-ridden feminism of our days. Yet, this is not the standard case of children rejecting the sins of parents in favor of those of a different nature which they personally choose to commit.

For once, at least, there will come a generation that shall not, as the Pharisees of old, be motivated to do good for the wrong reasons. And as our Lord put it, they will not build mausoleums for the prophets which their fathers rejected and killed, as a cover-up for the even greater prevarications of their own.

No longer will humanity correct past failings by present wrongs: the dialectical chain woven by the shuttle of time from one excess to its contrary abuse will have been broken. Casual sin, as a way of life for the many, will be no more. Mortal sin, if at all, will not be committed openly since lax standards of behavior will not be socially acceptable, not as a rule of Victorian prudery which denies what it cannot prevent, but as a commonality of opinion, as a chord of notes for a musician. The esthetic quality of virtue will be obvious.

That there will be saints as never before, however, does not mean that all will be saints. That is why the Church of Laodicea, the last Church in chronological terms, will eventually deserve the severe admonition:

"I know thy works; thou art neither hot nor cold...but because thou art lukewarm, and neither cold nor hot, I am about to vomit thee out of my mouth" (Apoc 3, 15-16).

This warning is addressed to a world on the verge of its commitment to Gog and Magog, the leaders of the final revolt of mankind against its Maker, after the release of Satan from his 1,000 years confinement in Hell.

The "beast . . . with two horns like a lamb and that spoke like a dragon" (Apoc 13, 11), Albrecht Dürer

VI

THE ANTICHRIST

This semi-paradise is one towards which nature itself, whether animate or inanimate, aspires as a prisoner does to freedom:

"For the eager longing of creation awaits the revelation of the sons of God. For the Creation was made subject to vanity - not by its own will but by reason of him who made it subject - in hope, because creation itself also will be delivered from its slavery to corruption into the freedom of the glory of the sons of God. For we know that all creation groans and travails in pain until now. And not only it, but we ourselves also who have the first-fruits of the Spirit - we ourselves groan within ourselves, waiting for the adoption as sons, the redemption of our body" (Rm 8, 19-23). The very freedom of the spirit turns to a benediction for matter, since matter is subject to spirit and will share in its glory, as it had shared in its curse: "Let the earth be cursed because of you" (Gn 3, 17). Theologians have assumed that Paul in Romans was describing metaphorically our material world on the dawn of its own dissolution at the end of the world. But this would have been contradictory. Nothing that is, would rather not be. Our world lives now, writes Paul, in the expectation of those better times which both matter and spirit will enjoy

45

once the "Kingdom... has come."[24]

As a corollary to this "glorious manifestation of the children of God, and of a creation liberated from the slavery of corruption," Msgr. Aldo Gregori thinks there should be a Return of Christ that will be both "physical and visible." For there is no Kingdom without a King and no Reign without a Ruler. And Gregori is here in disagreement with Iannuzzi who conceives merely of an Eucharistic presence of Christ...[25]

The least Christ could do is to show himself, for such an appearance was foretold by Paul in Hebrews (9, 28):

"Thus Christ, having been offered once to bear the sins of many, will appear a second time, not to deal with sin but to save those that are eagerly awaiting for him."

Strangely, the commentary of this verse in the Bible of Jerusalem is that this new and last manifestation of the Savior "will have no relation whatsoever with sin. Christians await the return in glory that will accompany the Judgment."

Once again, isn't this contradictory? For if this manifestation of Christ "will have nothing to do with sin," how can it have something to do with the Final Judgment?

Gregori, therefore, is justified in concluding that Christ, having already dealt with sin when he died on the Cross, will appear to those who are eagerly awaiting Him. He will answer the request of those very souls who were yearning for Him and saying: "Come, Lord Jesus" (Ap 22, 20).

---

24 According to the second law of Thermodynamics, there is entropy in matter, or what could be called a tendency to disorder or randomness. What is opposed to this trend, which physical science can measure and analyze, is what Teilhard de Chardin described metaphorically as an evolution of living creatures towards an always greater complexity.

25 See Msgr. Aldo Gregori: *La Venue intermédiaire de Jésus* (Parvis, CH-1648 Hauteville, 1997, p.49)

When will he return however? St. Paul mentions that he will not return quite as soon as many people seem to think. We shall be forewarned of his coming in more ways than one. Paradoxically, the most manifest sign will be the momentary triumph of the Antichrist, whose reign of evil he will bring to an end:

"Now concerning the coming of our Lord Jesus Christ and our assembling to meet him, we beg you, brethren, not to be quickly shaken in mind or excited, either by spirit or by word, or by letter purporting to be from us, to the effect that the day of the Lord has come. Let no one deceive you in any way, for that day will not come, unless the rebellion comes first, and the man of lawlessness is revealed, the son of perdition, who opposes and exalts himself against every so-called god or object of worship, so that he takes his seat in the temple of God, proclaiming himself to be God.

Do you not remember that when I was still with you I told you this? And you know **what is restraining him now** so that he may be revealed in his time. For the mystery of lawlessness is already at work; only **he who now re-strains it will do so** until he is out of the way. And then the lawless one will be revealed, and the Lord Jesus will slay him with the breath of his mouth and destroy him by his appearance and his coming. The coming of the lawless one by the activity of Satan will be with all power and with pretended signs and wonders, and with all wicked deception for those who are to perish, because they refused to love the truth and so be saved" (2 Thes. 2, 1-10: my emphasis).

The mood of these early Christians is significant. For them the return of Christ was nigh, as if it might happen tomorrow. Could they have been so deluded as to believe that the end of the world and the Last Judgment were as close as a forthcoming birthday? It was bad enough, seems to say St. Paul, that they should be awaiting for the intermediate return of Christ without taking into account the eventful episodes relating to the Antichrist who comes first.

Obviously the Thessalonians had misunderstood what Paul had told them in his previous letter:

"For you yourselves know well that the day of the Lord will come as a thief in the night. When people say, 'There is peace and security,' then sudden destruction will come upon them as travail comes upon a woman with child, and there will be no escape. But you are not in darkness, brethren, for that day to surprise you like a thief" (1 Thess. 5, 2-4).

Paul had been too optimistic, as he soon found out, and had to repeat to his readers in his next letter what he had already told them both *viva voce* and in writing. Lucky Thessalonians! Had they only recorded Paul's instructions as he was amongst them for their own and for our own benefit! We would not be pondering as to **whom** or **what** it is that will "restrain" for a while "the son of perdition." Theologians think that Paul was alluding to the Pope who will have to be discarded before "the man of lawlessness" can hold sway.[26]

---

26   Thus, it is in the very context of our lives that this could happen. Benedict XVI has recently retired. According both to the prophecies of Malachy and the announcement made by the Virgin to the visionaries of Garabandal, he is the last Pope within the span of the present "times" (the two thousand years) of our Church. That his end should be as dramatic as it seems to be portrayed in the Third Secret of Fatima is the tragedy awaiting us. Nothing will then stand in the way for the success of the long-ago schemed plot of subversion smithied in the secret havens of masonry. Lo and behold! Here is the false Messiah which, at first, to their confusion the Jews shall hail as Savior and which the rest of the world will gaze at in wonder: the Antichrist whose mellifluous tones, thanks to Internet, will reach to the very confines of the world. All the more that with English as the universal medium of communication, he will share the advantage

Whatever the case may be, we are dealing here with the Antichrist and not with Satan. For it is Satan who with his army as numerous "as the sand of the sea," "will attack the camp of the Saints and the beloved City," but only towards the end of time (Apoc 20, 8-9). By then, the Antichrist will already have been thrown into hell (Apoc 19, 20) since a thousand years. The Antichrist is he whose number (666) "is a man's number."

This number, however, can signify confusion. For, just as there have been many Antichrists in the course of history, such as Nero or Hitler, there is only one in our times who will deserve to be called by the name which was his until recently that of "the **Ante**christ": in other words, the one who comes **before** Christ. He precedes him like the night precedes the day. Nowadays, however, one had rather call him the **Anti**christ, because he is the counterfeit and contrary image of Christ.[27]

---

enjoyed by the builders of the Tower of Babel before the confusion of languages destroyed their unity of purpose. He will preach a humanistic gospel that would seduce angels if they were still fallible. Let us be on our guard! The Virgin has warned the Antichrist would be more eloquent than her own Son.

I suppose she means that he would sound more convincing to us than do the words of Christ, such as they are today, thrice removed from their original textuality, first by the process of memorization by the listeners, then by translation from Aramaic to Greek, and also by abbreviation when put down in writing.

Readers will be bound to expostulate that in my analysis I am not taking Pope Francis into account. The reason is simple. My manuscript was completed before Benedict XVI's retirement. I cannot comment about historical developments in the making. Among the prophecies concerning the end times, however, there is a certain "Peter the Roman" who is not accounted for in Malachy's list, as if he belonged more properly to a forthcoming epoch. It is tantalizing to speculate, in this respect, that Francis of Assisi, far

The nominal confusion resulting from this semantic diversity is a small one compared to the fact that this "son of iniquity" has, what we may call metaphorically, a twin brother. Both siblings are fathered by Satan, who in this spiritual fatherhood is not bound by limitations of time, since the second Antichrist will rule shortly before the end of the world. That is why such experts in eschatology as Robert Hugh Benson can evoke as Antichrist the seducer of mankind who will rule the world for a brief interlude before the Last Judgment. Now, this second "son of iniquity," deserves also to be called the **Ante**christ, since he comes before the second return of Christ. He should be even worse than his elder twin, since this will be Satan's last and ultimate fling on earth. I shall leave him, however, to the care of Benson, who is very good at describing him. I have enough of a task already dealing with the first and lesser Antichrist, who in his own right, is already a formidable figure.[28]

---

from calling him by this name, is supposed to have used the expression "Francesco di Pietro" to designate "Peter the Roman." But here, I am going out on a limb: the present is in the making.

27 Such is Satan's favorite strategy: send in a counterfeit image who, "as an angel of light," will respond to men's suspenseful awaiting of a messenger from heaven. Thus he had already in the 16th century provided a made-to-measure reformer for a Church badly in need of renewal. Spiritual energies, which would have been needed for a constructive task, were then diverted into a destructive jettisoning of what was good along with what was much in need of improvement. A "tabula rasa" ideal soon provided an outlet for dissatisfaction. And when an authentic reform came along with the Council of Trent, its benefit would only be felt in the 60 % of what remained of the Church.

28 According to Maria Valtorta, he deserves the following names: "Negation," "Evil in the flesh," "Horror," "Sacrilege," "Son of Satan," "Vengeance," "Destruction." This human embodiment of sin "will be a high-ranking personality, a star" among men. "Not a

Many theologians have been discussing at cross-purposes because of the confusion arising from this duality. That many exegetes have not been aware they were dealing with two of a kind is a cause for wonderment. But then, if Christ is to come twice, the devil is to be twice defeated, and serve two sentences in hell, once for a thousand years, and then for evermore.[29] When, as in both of these predicaments,

---

human star shining in a human heaven, but a star from a supernatural sphere, who, succumbing to the Enemy's flattery, will embrace pride after humility, atheism after faith, luxury after chastity, lust for gold after evangelical poverty, thirst for honors after a hidden life.

It is less frightening to see a star fall from heaven than to see this creature, already a 'chosen one', fall into the snares of Satan, and repeat the sin of his father of election... For a moment's pride the Antichrist, after having been a star in my army, will become the accursed and the obscure one." (Maria Valtorta as quoted by J.-P. Jouanneault: *Chrétiens magazine*, March 2012, p. 9). In the 13th century, a no lesser prophet than Francis of Assisi, had described him as an anti-pope, for he will not be "canonically elected" (as quoted by J.-P. Talbot, id. p. 20). Julie-Marie Jahenny (19-20 cent.) sees him issuing from a Muslim background, and more plausibly Mélanie Calvat, the visionary of La Salette, from a Jewish one.

29 The notion that there are "several antichrists" is not a new one, since it was proposed by St. John in his first epistle (2,18). Most biblical scholars, when they mention "**the** Antichrist," mean the one who will exercise his subversive activities shortly before the "end of time," *id est* the Last Judgment. I do not wish to disagree with this well-established opinion. Nonetheless, we should expect a no less convincing enemy of God, in that proximate future which the Virgin of contemporary apparitions designates as "the end of times." She calls this son of iniquity "the Antichrist" and warns us that he is already alive even though he has not yet revealed himself. At El Escorial, in Spain, on August 12, 1982, she told Amparo Cuevas: "The anti-christ finds himself in

he realizes that his time is short, he is energized by despair into conjuring up two replicas of the serpent of the earthly paradise, these two antichrists who will seduce, at one millenary of one another, even the elect themselves, if this were possible.[30]

---

my Church. He is among them. He has not yet revealed himself" (Gabriel: *Premier récit authentique des apparitions de l'Escorial*, F-X de Guibert; Paris, 1996, p.296).

Actually, we know far more about Antichrist No. I than we do about Antichrist No. II: the prototype is more familiar to us through the Apocalypse than the original. That is why exegetes such as Father Fessio in his book on "The Antichrist" who only took No. II under consideration, are, in my opinion, mistakenly attributing to this last figure much that does not pertain to him, but only to Antichrist Nr. I.

30 According to the Virgin of Kerizinen (1938-1965), two thirds of humans at that time were in a state of mortal sin. The situation can hardly have improved in the last fifty years. Who is the prophet that announced Satan would be released from hell sixty years before the end of the 20th century? This is when the war started which Satan would use as a cover-up for the extermination of the chosen people. For they are an object of hatred for him, both as the *Before Christ* two thousand year-old-vehicle for the transmission of Revelation, and, once they have converted, as apostles for the final preaching of the Gospel "unto the extremities of the world." The choices of God are "without repentance." So are those of Satan.

As far as the two Antichrists are concerned, according to Maria Valtorta, the situation is as follows, for we must distinguish between what will happen both at the **end of times** (pretty soon) and at the **end of time** (a thousand years later, shortly before the end of the world).

At the end of times, will come the Beast of the sea with the ten heads (the collective evil spirit as embodied in communism) and the Beast of the earth (the Antechrist or false prophet with Horns like a Lamb), while at the end of time it will be Satan himself, the

Antechrist number 2, who will be three times worse than number one, and accompanied by Gog and Magog (the evil nations). They will wage war against the elect.

Since Maria Valtorta's gift of prophecy has been established without a doubt for the past, for which her descriptions of the towns which Christ visited, her knowledge of biblical topography and of chronology of events have been confirmed by recent archeological findings, sightings and research, it must be said that her vision of the future is one with which we cannot do without.

Her assessment of the proximate future can be considered equally authoritative.

"When Christ will come to defeat his Adversary in the person of the Prophet, he will find very few persons marked in spirit with the sign of the Cross" (*I Quaderni*, vol I, p. 183).

Let me summarize to clear up all possible confusions. We have to deal with three monsters: first the fire-red Dragon, who threatens the Woman (the Church) and her children. He is a kind of reincarnation of the Serpent who seduced Eve. He is spiritually present in the Free-Masonry, which, as a covert body operating through its millions of members, is a collective entity. This seven-headed, ten-horned reptilian persona calls up from the sea a kind of replica of herself: the Beast. This Beast is a crossbreed of leopard, bear and lion all in one and yet has seven heads and ten horns. It stands for Communism. That is why "one of its heads seems to have a mortal wound." But since "its mortal wound [will heal]... the world [will follow] it with wonder." Read, dear Reader, and be amazed! For you are being warned that the much-heralded demise of Communism is but a momentary phase. As a Phoenix it will rise up again. We know how it treated the countries it held in its sway. What will it do when it rules the world? For it will owe much of its power to its ally, the Beast that rises "out of the earth" and that has "two horns like a lamb and [speaks] like a dragon."

For a detailed description of what this aberrant lamb will do, please read *Apocalypse* 13, 11-18. These 8 verses are weighted with such a density of meaning that any summary would be deceptive. As expected, this dragon-voiced creature is the

In the case now under consideration, which is the first return of Christ, we know that it is the Virgin, who as the New Eve, will crush the seducer beneath her heel.[31]

As I was saying earlier, after the night of confusion, comes the day of enlightenment. And St. Paul projects us into the future as if he were announcing a glorious event for tomorrow:

"Rejoice in the Lord always; again I will say, Rejoice. Let

Antichrist. He owes his powerful utterance to the media which he controls and the almost universal appeal of his soothe-saying. He will cancel, for the benefit of all, the age-old conflict between good and evil. This should come as a relief to our conscience-ridden humanity!

31 Unbeknownst to almost all theologians, she, the Virgin most pure, has already planted her dainty foot on this unseemly creature's head. Since he is a spirit, this is a metaphor. But his present-day frenzy has no other motive than this increasing threat against his liberty of action. Mary is appearing worldwide as she had never done before. And where she shows herself Satan is thrown into a fever of unrest. For she warns humans ahead and reveals his hidden plans. Thus at Medjugorje in 1981, nine years before the civil war in Yugoslavia. Or at Kibeho, also in 1981, eleven years before the genocide in Rwanda. And everywhere where visionaries, children, youths, women or even men, at Schio, Manduria, Garabandal, El Escorial, Cua, San Nicolas, Phoenix, Naju, etc..., announce forthcoming events in her name that souls may be saved before death can reap them with the sickle of God's wrath, the seven plagues of the Apocalypse, in which the evil spirits themselves play a part. For the Prince of this World is at work in war, pestilence, floods, earthquakes and all the disasters befalling a mankind whose sinfulness has delivered them to him as an easy prey. Hell on earth is the ultimate expression of a hatred for life whose objective can only be topped by the fiery furnace for lost souls in afterlife. The numberless Marian apparitions of today are an SOS call for prayer that can thwart the success of this final endeavor...

all men know your forbearance. The Lord is at hand" (Ph 4, 4-5)

He even prepares his young disciple Timothy for what he himself will not witness in person: "I charge you...to keep the commandment free and unstained until the apparition of our Lord Jesus Christ" (I Tm 6, 14).

In Paul's eyes, Timothy stands as a surrogate figure for future presbyters, who will read his epistle:

"But understand this, that in the last days there will come times of stress. For men will be lovers of self, lovers of money, proud, arrogant, abusive, disobedient to their parents; ungrateful, unholy, inhuman, implacable, slanderers, profligates, fierce, haters of good, treacherous, reckless, swollen with conceit, lovers of pleasure rather than lovers of God, holding the form of religion but denying the power of it. Avoid such people" (II Tm 3, 1-5).

When the prophets of old spoke of "the last days," they meant the messianic times, which is also an adequate expression for the first return of the Messiah. That Paul is evoking our own turn of the century is made even more obvious by the sequel (3, 6-7):

"For among [these people] are those who make their way into households and capture weak women, burdened by sins and swayed by various impulses, who will listen to anybody and can never arrive at a knowledge of the truth."

By these "weak women, burdened by sins and swayed by various impulses," Paul seems to be describing our feminists who live in untruth and whose conscience is "burdened" by their claim of the right to abortion.

Paul is not the only biblical author who is warning his readers to prepare for the second coming of the Lord. James, without sharing in the future detailed eschatological insights of John, does remind the Jewish converts of the diaspora that "readiness is all":

"Be patient... brethren, until the coming of the Lord. Behold, the farmer waits for the precious fruit of the earth... You also, be patient. Establish your hearts, for the coming of the Lord is at hand." (5, 7-8)

Patience is also the faculty of endurance. We will have a lot to suffer before the Lord is "at hand," either for his First or his Last Return..

In both cases, the night of tribulation must come before the light of day.

The suffering endured by mankind will be self-inflicted at first, if there is such a thing, since it will result from our own sinfulness.

Sin nurtures war, and war brings devastation and death.

And death leads to hell for so many, although it constitutes for the Martyrs a gate to Life.

In the state of a world, such as that of today, with Satan as its the Prince, the peace following the wars, will be a false peace initiated by the Antichrist.

He will take credit for it, however, just as he will enjoy reputation in the eyes of the many because of his wonders and pseudo-miracles.

Thus, it shall be for him the hour of earthy glory which he will reap for the three years and a half allotted to him for the persecution of the Church.

And then will come three days of darkness during which "stars will fall" and rid the world of its denizens of hell and all their followers.

One quarter of humanity will survive: the oft-quoted biblical "few."

Such at least will be the pattern of events preceding and following the First Return of Christ.

Once again immanent justice will have prevailed.

How often have we heard the complaint that the world is overpopulated and that drastic measures should be taken to prevent mankind's exponential increase!

Thus, it will be the prophets of doom who will be proven to be right, but at their own expense. For the promoters of birth-control and abortion will be especially targeted when the angels of God separate the chaff from the grain.

Willy-nilly, Man is maker of his own destiny.

One last remark for the benefit of those of our readers who will ask: "How can we recognize the Antichrist?" Besides his subversive doctrine, it might be a help to know that he will be a Semite, just as Christ was, but more distinctively, according to Marie-Julie Jahenny, an Arab rather than a Jew, a descendant of Ishmael.

It would be appropriate that he be so, since there is no greater scandal for a Moslem than the Mystery of the Trinity: "Who is the liar, but he who denies that Jesus is the Christ? This is the antichrist, he who denies the Father and the Son" (I Jn 2, 22). The obsessive way in which, in the Coran, the Trinitarian love in the heart of divinity is negated, points at Satan's attempt to register in history, as in an always growing collectivity, his own hatred. This rival Church whose membership is, through birthright, catching up with the Roman community in numbers, spoils for a revenge for the medieval crusades. Chesterton and Hilaire Belloc saw in Islam a greater peril for the West than Marxism. Islam, however, is too backwards to win, except in collusion with Communist countries.

We shall see... since no lesser authorities than Mélanie Calvat and countless other prophets claim that the Antichrist will be a Jew. But as we await for the worst we can enjoy the best, which is the present in which we are living. It is the "Tempus Mariae." She is appearing, the world over, as she has never done before. She is preparing us for the return of Christ even while she knows that, Satan, the Seducer of Mankind is at work in the world, as he too, has never done before. His human alter ego, the Antechrist must come first, as the concluding disaster afflicting mankind after two thousand years of an exponential Christianity.

Padre Pio, in his days, had warned us that the current apparitions of Mary, although they were authentic, would nonetheless not be received with the attention and the full veneration they deserve. As a result, what the Virgin has told would happen if her call to conversion remained ineffective, is about to take place. Mankind, inured to truth, will be receptive to lie. Padre Pio could add: "It is the false apparitions that will be taken as genuine."

What was he alluding to, if not to what had already been announced in the Gospels of Mark (13, 21-23) and Matthew (24, 23-27)?

"Then, if anyone say to you, 'Behold, here is the Christ', or, 'There he is', do not believe it. For false prophets and false Christs will arise, and will show great signs and wonders, so as to lead astray, if possible, even the elect. Behold, I have told it to you beforehand. If therefore they say to you, 'Behold, he is in the desert,' do not go forth; 'Behold, he is in the inner chambers', do not believe it."

Why is it that we should disbelieve these apparitions of Christ, if not that they will be those of the Antichrist? Masquerading as the Messiah, he will work wonders of a kind, real enough to seduce the majority of men. If Christ himself used miracles as proofs of his heavenly Mission so will the Man of Iniquity's reputation rest on unexplainable prodigies. He will seem to dispose of supernatural powers. It will be the devil, who enjoys in reality merely preternatural faculties, who will act through him. For the unsophisticated populace, however, magic can pass for miracle, and the devil's deceptions will readily be taken at face value. Let us beware!

VII

THE APOCALYPSE

In relation to the theory we are proposing, the New Testament can be considered as made of two unequal but complementary parts, the second of which is the *Apocalypse*. In terms of consistency alone, any disagreement or contradiction between them would be disturbing. This consistency can only be upheld if we resort, as often as possible, to the literal meaning of those many passages of the Scriptures which, only too often in the past, have only been understood metaphorically. We will have no difficulty in picking them out as we proceed, since at first reading they seem rather unbelievable.

Let us start with perhaps the most often quoted sections of the Apocalypse in chapters 12 and 13:

"And there appeared a great wonder in heaven, a woman clothed with the sun, and the moon beneath her feet; and upon her head a crown of twelve stars. And she being with child cried, travailing in birth, and pained to be delivered. And there appeared another wonder in heaven; and behold a great red dragon, having seven heads and ten horns... And the dragon stood before the woman which was ready to be delivered, for to devour her child as soon as it was born. And she brought forth a man child, who was to rule all nations with a rod of iron... And when the dragon saw that he was cast unto the earth, he persecuted the woman which brought forth the man child, who was to rule all nations with a rod of iron: and her child was caught up unto God; and to his throne. And the woman fled into the wilderness, where she had a place prepared of God, that they should feed her there a thousand two hundred and threescore days.... And the dragon was wroth with the woman, and went to make war with the remnant of her seed, which keep the command-ments of God, and have the testimony of Jesus Christ" (12, 1-6, 17).

"And I...saw a beast rise up out of the sea; having seven heads and ten horns, and upon his horns ten crowns... and the dragon gave him his power, and his seat, and great authority... And it was given unto him to make war with the saints, and to overcome them... And I beheld another beast coming out of the earth; and he had two horns like a lamb, and he spake as a dragon." (13, 1, 7, 12)

In spite of its symbolic character, the importance of this text should not be minimized. It reveals that our world is the showplace of a spiritual conflict, a war between angels, thrones and dominations on the dividing line between good and evil. This is a boundary which our human species has long since overstepped, and while the great dragon swept "a third of the stars from the sky and hurled them on the ground" (Apoc 12, 4),[32] it is today, according to the Virgin of Kerizinen (1938-1965), two thirds of humanity that are living in a state of mortal sin. Much worse is the assessment of Luz Amparo on Dec. 3, 2000:

"...I have seen that there are many souls, and I have even

---

32 According to mystics, this "one third of the stars of heaven" are the bad priests, bishops and cardinals.

been led to understand that this concerns almost one half of the world, that are possessed by the devil."[33]

This is a situation whose consequences should be disastrous in terms of natural catastrophes, plagues and wars. However, evil, as we know, is self-defeating, and God always prevails in the long run. God, furthermore, has a vested interest in our world, since his own Son was made man.

Another lesson to be drawn from this text, is that the woman in travail is the Church, whose progeny are the elect who can only escape death through persecution by the Beast by retiring in the desert. We are thus warned that salvation resides in a total withdrawal from a world ruled by the Antichrist whose reign is measured in time: "a thousand two hundred and a threescore days'. In other word, three years and a half.[34]

Gregori tells us that the resolution of the conflict de- scribed above is to be found in the Apocalypse (19, 20):

---

33   Luz Amparo Cuevas: Catéchèse à l'Escorial (Rassemble- ment à son image, Capelle, Onet le Château, 2013, p. 167). "According to one of the most famous demonologists in the world, the Italian Msgr. Corrado Balducci, the number of devils populating the earth should be reckoned at about two billion." (Editor's note, p. 176).

34   This does not mean that this text does not have more than one overlapping meaning. For instance, one which applies best is to be found in Hosea (2, 14 & 19-20):

.".. Behold, I will allure her, and bring her into the wilderness, and speak comfortably unto her.

... And I will betroth her unto me forever; yea, I will betroth thee unto me in righteousness; and in judgment, and in loving kindness, and in mercies.

I will even betroth thee unto me in faithfulness: and thou shalt know the Lord."

"...the beast was captured, and with it the false prophet," who is portrayed as "[that other] beast with the appearance of a lamb." These two are "thrown alive into the lake of fire that burns with sulfur." Soon after, in chapter 20, Satan himself, he who conjured up these incarnations of evil, is chained in turn "for a thousand years" and hurled after them into the same "bottomless pit."[35]

To him alone will release be given after a millennium, and then for a brief while. In this peaceful interlude of a thousand years, goodness can prevail. Men will owe this quasi-paradise to the Lamb who alone is worthy to open the scroll in the right hand of God:

"Worthy art thou to take the scroll and open its seals, For thou wast slain and by thy wound didst ransom men for God from every tribe and tongue and people and nation, And hast made them a kingdom and priests to our God, And they shall reign on earth" (Apoc 5, 9-10).

---

35 Thus no less than three entities are committed to hell, two of which forevermore, while the prime instigator of evil, the devil, will be entitled to a short reprieve in "a thousand years." Since Satan is the prince of confusion, he is presented in the *Apocalypse* in various "guises," and given various names. He is called "the ancient serpent" (12, 9) and the "great red dragon having seven heads and ten horns and upon his head seven diadems" (12, 3). He promotes a political and collective counterfeit of himself, the "beast that comes out of the sea, having seven heads and ten horns, and upon his horns ten diadems" (13; 1). This beast, who is a cross between a "leopard," a "bear" and a "lion," will be afflicted for a while with a curious handicap, because "one of its heads was smitten, as it were unto death; but its deadly wound was healed "(13, 2-3). It embodies communism, while the dragon cloaks more directly with iniquity his more immediate followers into his reptilians folds. These are the freemasons. As for the third beast, with horns like a lamb, it should be the false prophet, "the Antichrist."

This means that after the trials and tribulations resulting from the breaking of the seals, "those who had been slain for the word of God and for the witness they had bourne" will receive a new mission:

"And I saw thrones; and they sat upon them, and judgment was given unto them: and I saw the souls of them that were beheaded for the witness of Jesus, and for the word of God, and which had not worshipped the beast, neither his image, neither had received his mark upon their foreheads, or in their hands; and they came to life and reigned with Christ a thousand years.

But the rest of the dead lived not again until the thousand years were finished. This is the first resurrection. Blessed and holy is he that hath part in the first resurrection: on such the second death hath no power, but they shall be priests of God, and shall reign with him a thousand years" (Apoc 20, 4-6).

As Gregori remarks, a literal interpretation of this text has fantastic implications. It would mean that these saints and martyrs will live their beatific life with Christ in a novel way on this very earth, as resurrected persons, according to the pattern set on Easter day by their Savior himself. Furthermore, they will be spared the possibility of "a second death," *id est* damnation.

This is but one of the extraordinary events foretold in the Apocalypse. John had feared that some of his readers would react with skepticism. As far as present-day commentators and exegetes are concerned, he was certainly right. For their benefit, he issued a warning:

"I warn everyone who hears the words of the prophecy of this book: if any one adds to them, God will add to him the plagues described in this book, and if any one takes away from the words of the book of this prophecy, God will take away his share in the tree of life and in the holy city, which are described in this book" (22,18-19).

Therefore, it would be a mistake to downplay the urgency and the significance of this scriptural information. What John says may sound unbelievable, but hardly more so than what we read in Genesis. Creation *ab nihilo* is already so difficult a concept that modern science prefers to resort to the metaphor of the "Big Bang." Furthermore, the Fall of our first parents is so mysterious that Luther imagined it had been necessitated by God, while Darwinism reduced it to a mere myth. We know better, however, and we accept a dogma which accounts for the presence of evil in our world; and we say *"Felix culpa,"* since grace will more than overcome the consequences of sin. If we sinned in Adam, we are redeemed in Christ. Up to now, however, saints have been the exception, and sinners the norm, not to mention the damned whose proportion to the above mentioned two groups is difficult to assess. That this imbalance could be reversed in the future is so unthinkable that the *Apocalypse* has been read as much less than the "Good news" for which the Gospels stood. But with a literal reading of *Apocalypse* 20, 1-6, this text becomes for us a message of hope: we are assured virtue can be a collective accomplishment. This promise should become reality pretty soon: in a generation or two or hardly more. That is when Simone Weil's dismal comment, "le social, c'est le mal" will be refuted by the facts themselves.[36] No longer will a new Rousseau be able to proclaim that man was born good but was perverted by society. For if as before, man will be born afflicted by original sin, once cleansed by Baptism, he shall be upheld in righteousness by a supportive social surrounding. The King-

---

36 When Simone Weil says, "'What is social' is evil," she is speaking of public opinion, which, as we all know, is conditioned by prejudice & nurtured by the mimetic ascendancy of repetition.

dom of God will be both "within us" and "amongst us": in our hearts, and in the "civilization of love" (Paul VI) in which we live.

But if every Kingdom calls for a King, where will our Sovereign be?

"There's the rub" as Shakespeare would say. For if the coming of the Kingdom is announced explicitly in the *Apocalypse*, the Coming of Christ is merely implied.

Gregori's solution is that, since "there has always been an invisible presence of Christ in the Church," there should be a visible presence of his once his Kingdom has come (p. 68).[37] Since this presence of Christ is not clearly stated in the text, however, we must conclude that it will be as discreet and unobtrusive as his apparitions were in Jerusalem or Galilea after the resurrection. His followers alone benefited of them. But since after the "great tribulation," only the good will have remained, should not these manifestations occur even more often than after the Resurrection?

For the time being, our Savior having promised his Spouse, the Church, a destiny similar to his, we live in the expectation of her forthcoming Passion, or at least, less literally, of her trials and apparent death. This demise of hers should take place during the short reign of the Antichrist. Once she has revived, she should receive, in her convalescent state, visits from her Lord and Master similar to those she had enjoyed during the forty days preceding the Ascension. According to Gregori (p.69), Christ will show himself "once in one place, once in another, either to that particular soul, either to this whole community to redress, console and encourage the pursuit of holiness already in progress."

The Marian apparitions of our times in Medjugorje,

---

[37] *La Venue intermédiaire de Jésus dans les écrits du Nouveau Testament* (Ed. Du Parvis, Hauteville, Switzerland, 1997).

Garabandal, El Escorial, San Damiano, Cua or Schio, doubtless set the pattern for the apparitions we may expect from her Son in times to come. Mary precedes Jesus in all things, as the dawn announces the glory of the day. Her motherly concern is that we should be ready for the time when her son is there to exercise his tutorship of love, he whose "yoke is easy, [while] his burden is light" (Mt 11, 30).

This is how it should be, according to Saint Grignion de Montfort, since "it is through Mary that the salvation of the world began, and it is through Mary that it must be consummated."[38] Thus Mary, "in the second coming of Jesus Christ must be known and revealed by [the working of] the Holy Ghost." "Since she was the way through which Jesus came to us the first time, she will be also the way he comes the second time, though not in the same manner." Her very humility signals the defeat of Satan. And that is what the present-days apparitions of hers I have mentioned earlier are all about: seemingly, they set the pattern for her own Son. Those will be the times where holiness will not be the privilege of the very few. In the era of the Holy Ghost, after "the baptism by fire" of humanity announced by Marie des Vallées, charismata will abound. Their very multiplication already today signals that the falloff of the many assures to the remaining true believers a plentifulness of grace, as in the parable where the dutiful servant receives as a bonus the talent which the untrue servant had wasted. Tomorrow, therefore, such heavenly endowments as those of a Padre Pio will no longer be exceptional, even among laymen. The era of the Holy Ghost is a charismatic one. Mystics will abound.

The herald of this saintliness to come is Luisa Piccarreta

---

38 For the quotes of Louis-Marie Grignion de Montfort in this paragraph, see pages 514, 515 and 518 from his *Oeuvres complètes* (Ed. Du Seuil, Paris, 1966).

(1865-1947). Bedridden for sixty-four years of constant suffering, in a state of continual abstinence, this "Little Daughter of the Divine Will," as our Lord called her, left thirty-six volumes of that very doctrine of which she was the living embodiment. "And with her, in silence and obscurity, our Lord issued in the new Era of Grace, the true *Reign Of The Divine Will On Earth And the Fulfillment Of The Our Father:* may Your Will be done on earth as it is in Heaven."[39]

"She was the first to live in the Divine Will in the perfect imitation of the Humanity of our Lord: "My food is to do the Will of my Father"... and the perfect imitation of the most Holy Virgin: "Let it be done to Me..."[40]

The regeneration of humanity spearheaded by that of such Saints of the new era should go a long way to console the bleeding hearts of Jesus and Mary who are revealing themselves to us in their present-day apparitions.

What will, however, be the status of the common folk, these survivors of the winnowing process through which the angels will separate the chaff from the wheat? Can there be such a situation as a commonality of holiness?

In the broad sense of the word, certainly, for we will live to the full our status of children of God such as Saint Thérèse of Lisieux described it; and little children are endowed with the virtue of attachment to their Mother who embodies for them Providence. This trust is a holy estate.

Now comes the *crux oppositorum* which I am somewhat at a loss on how to resolve.

Little children seem incapable by their very nature of committing mortal sins to that very degree at which freedom

---

39   From the Introduction to Luisa's *When the Divine Will Reigns in Souls: Book of Heaven* (The Luisa Piccarreta Center of the Divine Will, Jacksonville FL, 1995 p. viii).

40   *Ibid.,* xix.

of choice is not yet theirs.

Thus virtue is the tribute man pays to God once he is capable of a responsible decision.

There is truly no reasonable alternative for him than to be virtuous.

Such was the conviction of Adam and Eve, until they encountered evil personified by the devil. At that very moment, innocence appeared as a burden no longer to be borne.

Out of this loss of innocence, concupiscence issued as a fruit from that very tree of knowledge of good and evil.

My question is: "If our first parents needed the devil to commit evil, will their descendants, once they have escaped from his influence during the thousand year interim that the devil will spend in hell, be spared all serious evildoing on their own?"

Mortal sin, after all, is what places man under the dominion of the Evil One.

Once evil, so to speak, has been placed under lock and key with its Maker, can a mere human perpetrate out of his own initiative an offense so serious as to deserve hell?

This riddle seems answerable by the question "no" if we take into consideration that it is only after the end of the devil's confinement in hell that a portion of humans, under the guise of God and Magog, will raise for the last time the banner of revolt against God.

During the happy Millennium of the reign of Christ, and of Satan's infernal sojourn, the necessary incentive for mortal sins should have been removed.[41]

---

41   To summarize the issue: to commit a mortal sin is to fall under Satan's spell. How could Satan; however, cast spells when he has been thrown "into the bottomless pit," in which he will remain confined "that he should deceive nations no more, till the thousand years be fulfilled..." (Apoc 20, 1-3). Is man, once left to

This does not mean that that perfection which is proper to Mary can be shared. Venial imperfections remain for the multitude.

On the other hand, I cannot help but conclude that the problem at hand is beyond finite intellectual capacities to resolve. Evil will forever remain a mystery for the human mind. This explains in part the unhealthy fascination it exerts, as if behavior could be patterned according to a new dimension. New vistas open in which to exercise our imagination. This absence of a good which should be there leads ultimately to madness, when it is the ultimate good which is at stake. The very confusion entertained by the idea that a substitute could be found for the good is aberrant. And Luther himself reached the apex of absurdity and blasphemy when he wrote: *Deus fecit bonum et malum* (God made [both] good and evil).

Lie is like a dream that is believable as long as it lasts. The awakening from the lie of sin is the process humanity will have to go through before it can reach the promised Land of the New Jerusalem. For such is the cue offered to the expectations of the pure of heart...

Conditioned as we are by the less than perfect society in which we live, it is difficult for us to conceive of a world in which the devil has no say. Once Satan is no longer there, how will we enjoy our newly found liberty centered on the exercise of charity?

To what degree can mere humans be considered blameless?

---

his own devices, capable of such intrinsic perversity as to choose hell instead of heaven, and hatred instead of love? If I knew the answer, would I put the question? When deliberate sin comes as unexpected as a singularity in physics, it turns almost into an object of speculation.

"A woman clothed with the sun, with the moon under her feet, and on her head a crown with twelve stars..." (Apoc 12, 1), Albrecht Dürer

VIII

THE PROPHETS OF OLD

The illustration of this happy state of affairs is to be found already in the Old Testament. That the prophets who announced the coming of the Messiah should have had, so to speak, an insider's knowledge of the twofold and contrasting character of His mission may appear unbelievable. It certainly caught the Scribes and Pharisees off balance. They were expecting a temporal reign which would outshine that of David and Salomon. They were not ready for the redemptive mission of a suffering Christ. In other words, they were putting the cart before the horse, and thought they could have a Kingdom of God on earth, not only according to their all-too earthly conception of worldly grandeur, but even before their own necessary conversion of the heart had taken place.

Let us therefore read the message of the prophets as it was meant to be understood. Now that the prophecies concerning "the suffering Christ" have been fulfilled, we know that the prophecies concerning the Coming of the Kingdom are believable. We can rejoice in them without an afterthought.[42]

---

42 We owe the nine follcwing headings to Joseph Iannuzzi.

First, evil will lose its appeal to man or its sting in nature:

"All who are alert to do evil will be cut off..." (Is 29,20). This means that those who are intent to do good will remain.

"The beast of the earth you need not dread. You shall be in league with the stones of the field and the wild beasts will be at peace with you" (Jb 5, 22-23).

The wolf and the young lamb will feed together" (Is. 65,25).

If the carnivorous animals no longer prey on the herbivorous ones, could it be by implication that man will no longer eat meat, but be content, as in paradise, with the fruits of the trees and the produce of his own garden?

Or more precisely, if "the lion is to eat grass with the lamb," should this metaphor not apply to the nations at last at peace with one another?

Second, women will no longer suffer from the full impact of the afflictions laid upon Eve:

"Raise a glad cry, you barren one who did not bear..." (Is 54,1).[43]

"See, I come to you... I will settle crowds of men upon you... cities shall be repeopled; and ruins rebuilt. I will settle crowds of men and beasts upon you, to multiply and be fruitful. I will repeople you as in the past; and be more generous to you than in the beginning; thus you shall know that I am the Lord" (Ez 36, 9-11).

---

43 According to Maria Valtorta, sexuality will no longer bear the stigma of shame it owes to its animality: "God had not intended that man and woman give life in the same way as do animals or plants... Man and woman will find anew the mode of procreation which guarantees the superiority of the soul to the body..." (As quoted by Samuel de Montaudoux: *Prophéties pour le 21 e siècle*; Résiac, Montsûrs, 1994, p. 123).

Third, creation will be as reborn:

"For behold, I create new heavens and a new earth, And the past will not be remembered..." (Is 65,17).

"Her deserts he shall make like Eden; her wastelands like the garden of the Lord." (Is 51; 3).

"'This desolate land has been made into a garden of Eden,' they shall say." (Ez. 36,35).

Fourth, the righteous will rule. They should have always done so, but power has traditionally been such a magnet for the unrighteous, that the wicked have prevailed only too often; But it will not be so in the time to come:

"My chosen ones shall inherit the land" (Is 65,9).

"We will be made just and holy" (*Epistle of Barnaby*).

Fifth, good health will assured:

"No more shall there be... an infant that lives but a few days, Or an old man who does not fill out his days; To die a hundred years old will be to die young, [while] not to live for a hundred years will be a sign of malediction" (Is 65, 20).

"Then will the eyes of the blind be opened, the ears of the deaf be unstopped; Then the lame will leap like a stag and the tongue of the dumb sing"(Is 35, 5-6).

Sixth, the Lord will be praised as never before:

"Then the Lord's name will be declared on Zion, the praise of God in Jerusalem, when all peoples and kingdoms gather to worship the Lord" (Ps 102, 22-23).

"I come to gather nations of every language, they shall come and see my glory" (Is 66, 18).

"From one new moon to another, and from one Sabbath to another, all mankind shall come to worship before me, says the Lord" (Is 66,23).

Seventh, the light of day will be renewed:
"The light of the moon will be like that of the sun and the light of the sun will be seven times greater…" (Is 30,26).
"I will turn darkness into light before them" (Is 42,16).

Eighth, we can expect an agrarian utopia:
"They shall live in the houses they build, and eat the fruit of the vineyards they plant… and my chosen ones shall long enjoy the produce of their hands. They shall not toil in vain" (Is 65, 21-23).

Ninth, a Royal Priesthood is announced:
"You yourselves shall be named priests of the Lord, ministers of our God you shall be called" (Is 61, 6).
But here, we have to call on the New Testament, for more information on the subject. We could have done so for most of the previous sections, but repetitive quotes may appear redundant.
"…You are a chosen race, a royal priesthood, a holy nation, a people of his own, so that you may announce the praises' of him who called you out of darkness into his wonderful light" (I Pt 2,9).
"Blessed and holy is the one who shares in the resurrection. The second death has no power over these; they will be priests of God and of Christ and they will reign with him for the thousand years" (Apoc 20,6).

And since I am a romantic soul, I will say that there will be no more mismatched marriages since couples will be led to one another, as was the case for the parents of Thérèse of Lisieux, by spiritual affinity rather than passionate inclination.
Furthermore, if we are to believe Zechariah, the Jews will be more especially instrumental in the conversion of the

world: "In those days ten men of every nation, speaking in different tongues, shall take hold, yes, take hold of every Jew by the edge of his garment and say, 'Let us go with you, for we have heard that God is with you" (8,23).

Why should we take all these promises of the Old Testament as literally as we hear them expressed above?

To this question, we have a ready answer: we take them literally, because the Church Fathers did so. And the Church Fathers did so, because that is the way the Apostles themselves interpreted the Old Testament, when they applied its prophecies to the New Jerusalem, our Catholic Church. These Fathers merely followed, for the second Coming of Christ, that very method of interpretation of texts of the Old Testament which the Apostles had used when they quoted the prophets or the psalms to prove that Christ was truly the long-awaited Messiah.

Did not Christ say to his apostles after his resurrection: "These are the words which I spake unto you, while I was yet with you, that all things must be fulfilled, which were written in the law of Moses, and in the prophets, and in the psalms concerning me"? (Lk 24, 44).

If therefore the prophecies which announced a suffering Christ have been fulfilled, so must those who concern his glorious Reign on earth receive their accomplishment.

As a clincher, let me quote Isaiah, describing, in nuptial terms, a mystical relationship between humanity and its creator:

"For now your Creator will be your husband; His Name: Yahweh Sabaoth" (54, 5).

When there is a meeting of mind between God and his creature, what ensues is happiness enough:

"Seek ye first the Kingdom of God, and his righteousness; and all these things shall be added unto you" (Mt 6, 33).

"These things," according to the context are all those which men need to live without having the worry about the morrow.

Our Lady of the Escorial

IX

THE ROLE OF MARY & THE SAINTS

As far as Mary's role in the "end time" will be, this is what Joseph Iannuzzi has to say:

"Since Mary's maternity came by the power of the Holy Spirit for the purpose of generating and forming the Son of God, the Church bestows upon her the title 'Mother of the Church' to illustrate the continuity of her mission of generating and forming other sons of God."[44]

Our greatest authority on the subject, however, is Saint Louis Grignion de Montfort:

"Towards the end of the world... Almighty God and his holy Mother are to raise up great saints who will surpass in holiness most other saints as much as the cedars of Lebanon tower above little shrubs."

"The formation and education of [these] great saints... are reserved to her."

"In the second coming of Jesus Christ, Mary must be known and openly revealed by the Holy Spirit..."

"She will extend the Kingdom of Christ over the idolaters and Muslims, and there will come a glorious era when Mary

---

44 Rev. Joseph Iannuzzi: *The Splendor of Creation* (St. Andrews Productions, McKees Rocks, PA, 2004, p.84).

is the Ruler and Queen of Hearts."[45]

This last sentence of Louis Grignion de Montfort is an almost literal quotation from Blessed Mary d'Agreda. As for Saint Maximilian Kolbe, he tells us that:

"The image of the Immaculate will one day replace the large red star over the Kremlin..."[46]

She is indeed the Morning Star, the one who goes on shining when the sun is there. Without Mary, there is no rule of Jesus. Did she not announce in her Magnificat the coming of the Kingdom of God? For she prophesied that "the proud" would be "scattered," "the mighty" dethroned, and "the rich" sent away empty-handed, while the "lowly' would be "exalted, the "hungry" "filled with good things," and "Israel, his servant..." "helped." Indeed, the Church is the heaven-chosen substitute of Israel in the fulfillment of the latter's mission as the shepherd of all Nations. Thus it is in the second part of the "Magnificat," that Mary responds with a hymn of praise to the theme outlined in the words of the Angel: "He shall be King over the House of Jacob forever."

Once invested, he will rule through his Saints. As said previously, this is literally what will take place (Apoc 20,4). Lo and behold, Saints will hold sway over saints: Those who were washed in the blood of Lamb, will come back to life in "the first resurrection" for this very purpose. And it can be said astonishingly, that they will exercise their spiritual sovereignty over souls even greater than their own. As this life of ours is the pale shadow of the one hereafter, and stands almost as a metaphor for the real thing, the holiness of yesterday is a mere sketch for the completed picture the Supreme Artist has in mind. God has staged states of

---

45 Men will then find themselves in the fellowship of angels as the servants of Mary, as Grignion de Montfort was during his life.
46 *Id.* Pp. 83-84.

perfection in the course of time, as in the steps of a staircase. Just as the faith of Abraham, though it was that of a man imperfect in other respects, ushered in the people of God, yet it would be outclassed by the virtue of Joseph, the advisor of the Pharaoh. At a later date would come Moses who would deserve to be called "the most perfect of men." But this prophet did not attain the full spiritual stature of a St. John the Baptist, of whom Christ said that "among sons of women, none had been greater" (Lk 7, 28). And yet, this precursor of Christ would be dwarfed by "the least in the kingdom of God," said Christ. But of which "kingdom of God" is He speaking? Is it that which He established through His own death and resurrection? In that case, the disciple whom Jesus loved should outshine his namesake. According to St. Grignion de Montfort, however, once the Kingdom comes into its plenitude, Christ and his holy Mother shall raise up, as said before, "great saints who will surpass in holiness most other saints as much as the cedars of Lebanon tower above little shrubs."

In terms of perfection the sky is the limit. The whole history of mankind, after the Fall of Adam, is a slow process of return to its initial stage; but only seemingly. For through the merits of Christ, the resulting sanctification, by its achievements, will surpass in dignity that of our forefather in his state of innocence. The Church grows, through its most eminent members, to the full stature that its spousal relation deserves, in a mysterious analogy with the stages of mystical life. Israel, who preceded her, could be termed to have lived in the *via purgativa*. In its first two thousand years, the Church of Peter suffered and flourished in the *via illuminativa*, on her way into the ultimate millennium, where she reaches her goal, the *status unionis*. This parallel illustrates in three successive steps the access to perfection of her only truly successful children: the Saints.

This is meant as a figurative formulation, and not as a doctrinal elucidation. For the Church as such has always shared in the perfection of her head, Christ. But in her children, in a providential way, she has never ceased to grow. And if a Saint Theresa of Avila, just to mention her, certainly reached a "status unionis," there remained still, in this very summit of spiritual life, the possibility of a breakthrough onto a higher level. This apparently limitless access to "the height, the width and the depth" of charity, in a never-ending becoming, from what seemed tentative at first, to the perfection reached by a further generation of mystics, evokes the infinity of afterlife where the soul goes from one discovery to the next in her contemplation of God.

As already mentioned in previous chapters; the forerunner of this new holiness is Luisa Piccarreta (1865-1947). A victim-soul, she can be compared to Maria Valtorta, even though the deep knowledge she imparts is not that of Christ's life and works, but that of "The Life of the Divine Will." This "Little Daughter of the Divine Will" would teach us that there is no perfection beyond this exemplary "fiat." This achievement will not only be that of a future generation of individual Saints, but also, in collective terms, that of the body of faithful in the Kingdom of the Divine Will whose advent is at hand.

Let us listen to what Christ says to Luisa:

"I come as King among the peoples... I wish only one thing: that my will reign amongst you." And Christ announces, even before their recent multiplication, the Marian apparitions:

"My Celestial Mother... comes... midst the nations to prepare them to receive the sovereignty of the reign of my will." The saintliness which will then reside in so many will be "divine and non human": it will be such that these suns of holiness "will eclipse the most beautiful stars of the saints of preceding generations. That is why I intend to purify the earth, unworthy as it is now of these prodigies of sanctity."

What I summarize here in a few lines, Luisa thematizes again and again in the 36 volumes Jesus dictated to her.

This message is prophetic. Since "the worst chastisement is the triumph of the wicked," their very success today is part of the strategy leading to the purification of God's Church, as it suffers persecution in their hands. Once these minions of Satan have served their purpose, however, God "will disperse them as dust in the wind."

**The hymn in adoration of the Lamb (Apoc 14, 1-5),
Albrecht Dürer**

X

THE PROPHETS OF TODAY

"Do not despise prophecies" (I Thess 5 ,2)

"Assuredly the Lord God does nothing without revealing his secret to his servants the prophets" (Amos 3, 7). These are honored and revered, but usually only after their death. A prophet is a voice raised in the wilderness. And in our times, what a wilderness! Never have there been so many messengers from Heaven as today, nor proportionately so few with a following! From among our contemporary announcers of things to come, let us mention those who have nonetheless had perhaps the greatest influence: Don Stefano Gobbi, Vassula Rydén and Luz Amparo Cuevas. Not to forget Maria Valtorta ("The Story of the Man-God") whom Christ called upon through his revelations to fill the gaps in the recital of his words and doings in the Gospel, the veracity of which can readily be ascertained by this visionary's encyclopedic knowledge in matters of chronology, astronomy, archeology, biography, etc...: a knowledge which staggers the mind on the part of a cripple confined to bed and with no access to a library, or for that matter bound to the time-bound limitations of discoveries which historians made only after her death. I will quote her extensively later.

Don Stephano Gobbi published the messages he

received from the Virgin in the *Blue Book* he wrote for the Marian Movement for Priests:

"...the end of times and the coming of Jesus in glory are at hand," says Mary, who lists as follows "the signs described in the Holy Scripture" concerning this event. "The first sign is the widespread diffusion of errors... The second one is the outbreak of wars and fratricidal conflicts... The third is the bloody persecution of those who remain faithful to Jesus and his Gospel...

The fourth sign shall be the horrible sacrilege, committed by... the Antichrist" (31.12.1992).

Since the first sign, the almost universal abandonment of orthodox belief in its integrity, even among so-called Catholics today, plus the collective apostasy of previously Christian nations, is as obvious as the ominous rumblings of forthcoming wars, there is but little time left for "those who remain faithful to Jesus and his Gospel" to prepare for martyrdom.

"I am especially close to the Church in these last times where she will have to live the bloody hour of her purification and her Great Tribulation. For she too must the Eternal Design of the Heavenly Father be accomplished, and it is thus that she is called to climb the Calvary of her own immolation. My very beloved daughter will be struck and wounded, and led to the gibbet where she will be crucified. The ungodly Man will enter into her bosom and bring to its peak the abomination of the desolation announced in the Holy Scriptures" (Jan 1, 1994).

"...the two-horned Beast alike to a Lamb stands for the Freemasonry which has infiltrated my Church, i.e., the ecclesiastical Freemasonry which has spread more especially among the members of the Hierarchy" (June 13, 1989).

With all this, **Vassula Rydén** concurs, as if it were contrastingly. This wife, mother and orthodox mystic is the scribe through whose hand she claims Christ conveys the following messages:

"I prepare for you a new Heaven and a new Earth full of the fruits born from the Tree of Life... I will come soon to purify you..." (16, 8, 88)

This semi-Eden will results from "the second Advent of the Lord, which is the second Pentecost" (24.4.90).

"Love will return as Love" (9.7.1991).

"The head of Satan will be crushed beneath the heel of my Mother. But be of courage, because a fire will come before my day... a fire without which the face of the earth could not be changed" (19.9.91).

"Entire nations shall be wiped out... When the hour of darkness comes, ... I will make you see your soul as it is; and when you see that it is as black as coal,... your anguish shall be so great that you have never felt such a distress before, [and you will be made aware] that your own perfidy is much greater than the [pitch] darkness around you..." (18.2; 93).

"The hour shall come when men of power will enter into my Sanctuary, men who do not come from me... The Pope will have much to suffer" (17.3.93)

As for **Luz Amparo Cuevas**, this Spanish mother of seven saw the Virgin or Christ and repeated their messages. We are warned that a worse chastisement than the deluge is on its way and that "The final Judgment of Nations is near" (B.V.,15.1.1982).

"My Son," says the Virgin, "will come down on a white cloud, surrounded by angels" (14.1.83)... "with his great power and great majesty"(B.V., 21.11.1982).

"The Day of Yahweh is near," says Christ. "One should do what is necessary to find oneself on the right side with my elects so as to be removed into the promised land" (O. L.,

19.3.92).

On the nature of this "removal," our Mother Mary supplies more information:

"The celestial vessels are ready to transport the elects onto the promised land. These vessels will come surrounded with a blue light like a kind of cloud"... (B.V., 24.2.83).

"The chariots of fire of God the Father are ready, my children, to transport you... But be attentive: you are many who are called sons of God, but few will be the elects..." (B. V., 3.9.83).

"...those who are elected will remain as in ecstasy; nothing will affect their bodies" (B. V. 21.4.84).

One of Luz Amparo's favorite themes, or should we say of our Lady's, is the marking of the sons of God with a seal on their forehead. Let none of them fall into the sin of presumption, however, for this seal will be of no help if they do not observe the commandments. All the while, Satan, forever a simulator, will stamp his followers on the forehead or on the hand with his own seal, the number 666.[47]

---

47 While the purpose of this mark of damnation sealed on head or hand is clear to all, and should make would-be sinners pause before they irretrievably commit themselves to a fellowship with the devil, the mark of election seems to me far more mysterious. For the latter is invisible, while the former mark should be as obvious as a pass-card for a hotel-room. Needless to say, the rooming facilities should give the lie to the expectations of the heedless guests. On the other hand, the invisible token of God's delight in the company of good men is a gift of the Spirit that can be jettisoned with a single mortal sin. The Capitals O. L. Stand for our Lord, and B. V. for the Blessed Virgin.

Our references: Gabriel, *Premier récit authentique des apparitions de l'Escorial* (F. X. de Guibert, Paris, 1996) and Association Vierge de Douleurs du Pré Neuf de l'Escorial, *L'Escorial, Messages 1992-1998* (F-64170, Artix).

In one respect at least, our Lord contradicts somewhat Iannuzzi's, and our own expectations. For his Return will not be as discreet as his subsequent Presence should be:

"I will come with glory, but I will not leave my Cross behind. And this sign will be seen from all parts of the world. I will come full of glory and with armies of angels... Look! What a beauty, my daughter... look at my power and my majesty..." (O. L. 5.3.94)

Luz Amparo is truly prophetic in the tradition of John in his Apocalypse. What she describes is a Parousia fittingly suggestive of the one that will bring, at a later date, our world to an end:

"I am God and men do not see me as God, and since I am God,... I will come to purify the earth. As gold is refined, so shall I purify men. I will bring fire to the earth and it shall burn entirely...

I shall have the grain removed from earth; I shall have the grain placed in the granary and I shall set fire to the chaff... (3.12.94).

And the smoke from this bonfire of wicked souls shall darken the world for three days..." as we shall see in next chapter.

"The Great harlot ... siting on a scarlet beast ... drunk with the blood of the martyrs of Jesus" (Apoc 17, 1-7), Albrecht Dürer

XI

THE GREAT TRIBULATION[48]

"For then, there will be a great tribulation, such as has not been from the beginning of the world until now, nor will be" (Mt 24, 21).

With Luz Amparo of El Escorial we are dealing with a prophet whose messages from the Virgin or from Christ (1981-1998), in contrast to those of the four visionary girls of Garabandal (1961-1965), were favorably received by the local Church authorities. Yet, the messages from Heaven in both places have much in common. Alas, it is only too often that the reaction of the local bishop appears unexpected and distressing to the average Marian Devotee!... [49] It is a fact of common observation, however, that the contents of messages of the Virgin in most of the recent places of apparitions, whether they have been officially approved, or treated

---

[48] Nota bene: In this complex chapter, even though the footnotes were meant, as always, to complement the main text, they can also be read afterwards as a whole, as a clarifying summary of the topic at hand. *This is a clue for easy reading.*

[49] The diversity of the rules of discernment invoked, from one bishop to another, go a long way to explain the discrepancies observed.

with benign neglect, merely tolerated or much criticized, openly encouraged or eventually condemned[50]... are all substantially the same. This is true in spite of the great diversity of visionaries involved.

A consensus can be reached, therefore, on what information Heaven *in persona Mariae*, or other messengers of the Holy Ghost intend to convey to the faithful. I am listing here, on the most obvious themes, what should be of interest to most of us. Thus what follows is what "our Lady of the Apocalypse" has to say to our generation, and what events she announces for the future. We describe them tentatively, according to their presumable chronology.[51] According to the Madonna, the present-day decline of wildlife, whether in the seas or the skies, is a portent of what is to come. We who with our insecticides, have stilled the songs of our feathered friends or banished them from the skies, should know what to expect from a nature we have savaged.

Here is a list of what we should be expecting:

1) A **mega-earthquake**, with attendant tsunami, and the damage they will occasion, especially on the East Coast of the United States.

---

50 "Eventually condemned": I am not evoking here all places of apparitions where this was the case, but only those for which, hypothetically, this condemnation might be rescinded in the future. In the past, for instance, this has already taken place at Heroldsbach whose visionaries were excommunicated for eighteen years (1949-1967) and which is now recognized as a Center of Re-evangelization.

51 Obviously, there will be much overlapping of events, especially for numbers eight to twelve. Thus the rate of the economic collapse is not foreseeable, even though the likelihood of such a crisis is obvious even to prophecy-skeptics.

2) A year in which there will be two spring-times, but not as a promise of a double harvest. The first spring will be interrupted by a worldwide cold-wave of a low as minus 30, presumably as a result of volcanic eruptions that will darken the heavens with clouds of dust. Such a disaster, on a smaller scale, has already happened in the nineteenth century following the eruption of the Tambura (Indonesia: 1815). Famine ensued worldwide in the following year.

3) Winds of such an intensity that they "will blow away whatever stands in their path," and for which present-day tornadoes or typhoons seem small-scale trial runs.

4) A heat-wave of such unprecedented intensity that the surface of the earth will be scorched brown.[52] Is it on this occasion that food will be so scarce that cannibalism will be practiced? Should this dry-spell be the one announced in the Apocalypse (11, 3-6) where it is related to the inter-vention of the "two witnesses" who prophecy "for a thousand two hundred and sixty days"? "Have [they not] the power to shut heaven, so that it will not rain during the days of their prophesying?" Tradition has it that these two witnesses are either Elias and Enoch or Moses and Elias..

Whatever was man's direct or indirect responsibility in these catastrophes resulting from climate-change, the following events will result directly from our sins:

---

52 For items 1-4, see *L'Illumination des consciences* of Sulema (Parvis, Hauterive, Switzerland, 2013), as quoted in *Stella Maris* (id., Jan. 2013, p. 27-28).

5) Thus, as an opener, it seems appropriate to mention the prophecy of Sister Faustina, to whom Christ had said:

"Before coming as a righteous Judge, **I [will] come first as King of Mercy**. Before the advent of the day of justice, a sign in the sky will be given to men. All light will go out in the sky, and there will be great darkness on all of the earth. The Sign of the Cross will appear in heaven, and from the wounds in the hands and the feet of the Savior, a great light shall stream, which for a while will illuminate the earth."[53]

The Cross of Jesus is our consolation. At least it is one for the elect, while it is a sign of rejection for who is on the way to hell. Thus it seems appropriate as a first test of men's consciences, even though its timing is most uncertain and could fit just as appropriately as the closing episode of our eschatological future.

The actual event it evokes is that of a four-fold division among the witnesses of the Passion of Christ: those close at

---

53   Sister Faustina was very reluctant at first to transmit this information which she foresaw would be received with much skepticism. But our Lord insisted that if she did not do so, she would be personally responsible for a resulting loss of souls. She was not the only one to whom God confided this mission. At Dozulé (France: 1970-1978), for instance, the visionary Madeleine Aumont announced that the Sign of the Cross would appear in the sky as a forbidding omen of the Judgment to come: "If Man does not raise the Cross, I will make it appear, but there will no longer be time left." This was a conditional warning, following the request that a giant cross of 738 meters high (the altitude of the Golgotha) be erected at this point of earth in Normandy. I interpret the discrepancy between this message and the plausibility of its being taken into consideration as the foreboding proof that Heaven is aware that our time is running out. Practically speaking, such ominous words are a lesson to be understood in retrospect.

Calvary who shared in spirit the agony of Mary and the grief of John; the apostles who fled in distress; the bystanders who did not take sides and lastly the Pharisees and Sadducees who rejoiced at what they saw. In the context of the eschatological occurrence evoked above, however, indifference or satisfaction are hardly conceivable, while reassurance, repentance, awareness or rejection are more likely. Woe to them, however, who, against all evidence, reject the "Sign in the Sky," for such is the call to repentance that should usher, a few days later, a worldwide event of even greater magnitude - but this chronological order is speculative on our part.[54]

A mysterious psychological phenomenon should strike, at that very moment, each and every human. It will be given to them to see with perfect clarity the actual state of their own conscience and the nature and number of their sins.[55]

---

[54] Nothing is more difficult to foretell than the timing of supernatural wonders. From other sources this vision of Christ on the Cross for all to see is the close or immediate prelude to the "three days of darkness" that will bring about the total destruction of our civilization of sin.

[55] This has been announced, not only at places of apparitions such as Garabandal, El Escorial and Emmitsburg, but also by Saint Faustina, as the supreme attempt of God's mercy to recapture the lost sheep. People have been known, in near-death experiences, to have perceived, in what seemed an instant, the whole course of their life, or in moral terms, the complete list of their failings. This apprehension of what has been, or what should not have been, is the immediate recollection of the past, triggered by the urgency of the situation. In the same way, the perception of a looming universal disaster will impact upon the *psyche* of all humans a clear knowledge of all what they have done wrong. There will be signs in the sky for all to see, a momentous planetary menace and men will moan as a woman in travail. When "time is out of joint" and electromagnetic fields are disturbed to the point no car can

This inner revelation will be triggered, according to some present-day prophets - for instance Mama Rosa of San Damiano - by the ominous approach of a comet.[56] Its size and its proximity to the earth will provoke terror, as a threat of instant destruction. It will furthermore introduce a paralyzing perturbation in our worldwide and private electronic communications and in the distribution of electric power. For such should be the case.

"As soon as you see the heaven darken, get on your knees, rosary in hand, and pray, pray, pray, since all will happen very fast. Day will turn to night; as in Fatima, the sun will rotate, and lose its light for three hours; the moon will darken and many phenomena will be visible all over the earth! ...people will think the end of the world is at hand... For everyone it will be as a mystical experience during which he will perceive the state of his soul in the light of divine

---

run, no plane can fly and, presumably, no computer can perform, then all of humanity will be made aware, as King David was, to what extent it had "sinned against the Lord" (II Samuel 12, 13). One of the best formulations of the Warning is that of a contemporary visionary, Maria, as reported in *Le sourire de Marie* (Montsûrs, France; June-July 2012, pp. 54-57): "O my little ones, the Father, in his great wisdom, will allow, at the time of the Warning, each one of His Children to see the state of his soul, the number and the horror of his sins as well as the repercussions such sins have had for all creatures and for the whole world. He will also make you perceive to what persistence in evil will lead if you persist in evil and in your stubbornness: heaven or hell eternally." Since "the comet of the Warning is on its way," this will be "for many the ultimate occasion for their conversion."

56 Or by the collision of two heavenly bodies, according to Conchita of Garabandal, and other prophets, as a result of which impact a cross-like sign of cosmic dimension will appear in the sky.

Justice, similarly to the grace granted to Saul of Tarsus..."[57]

While the star of Bethlehem came as a herald of peace and joy, this unexpected visitor from outer space will instill quite different feelings. While it should spur good Christians to penance and prayer and shake lukewarm believers out of their complacency, it will also bring about the conversion of many sinners. It is expected, however, that it shall drive hardened evildoers, either into a Judas-like despair, or into a frenzied revolt which bodes ill, not only for themselves, but for their fellowmen. We observed in our times, for instance, that Hitler resorted to the Jewish genocide in 1942, as soon as it became obvious, even to him, that he would lose the war. Evil is accomplished for evil's sake once its accomplishment cannot bring anything else but an increase of evil, even unto the person or persons involved. Such is the sinister logic of total despair, the circularity of wickedness in which the "pre-damned" soul entraps itself by the commission of always more heinous crimes.[58] What is bad turns into absolute evil when what is good seems to have fled beyond recall.

The other side of the coin is that conversions will be so plentiful following the Warning that there will be a rush on confessionals in which priests will have to be on call day and night.

The Warning will announce the Theophany of the Judgment of Nations. As far as the Warning is concerned, it can also be called an Illumination of the conscience. For whoever is in the state of grace, what a cause for rejoicing! But for whoever is not, what a call for conversion! Just as the

---

57 According to Sulema in *L'Illumination des consciences* (Parvis; Switzerland as quoted in *Chrétiens Magazine*, Dec. 2013, p, 26).

58 "The sin against the Holy Ghost will not be forgiven either in this world, nor in the next" (Mt 12, 31)

rejoicing, however, cannot be merely reassuring, because it will be accompanied by the clear knowledge of one's failings, the conversion cannot be automatic, because men remain free to decide. Among the 7 billion denizen of this world, this trial by truth should result in a division as decisive, breathtaking and dramatic as that which took place at the Fall of one third of the angels, even if it is not as instantaneous. Since we are as beings less perfect than angels, it can be assumed that the quota of election should be smaller in our case, perhaps by one third. Yet, even if all of mankind perished at the time of Noah, with the exception of one family, this does not mean that of those who drowned because of their sins, quite a few did not repent in time. For the latter, the trial by water was to be their way of salvation, while mankind stands now on the eve of a trial by fire that will be equally selective.

Men should be properly warned of the Warning, however, since at that time those who are not in the state of grace will be struck unaware by this thunderbolt of truth from which many will die. "Readiness is all," and it is our fraternal duty to spread the news of this forthcoming illumination of consciences, which will be as sudden as lightning, and as fearsome as an execution. It is difficult to say how many, as a consequence, will find themselves in hell before they had the time to repent. For such is the place ready-made for those who least expect its existence, or in other words who have lived as if there were no afterlife. The survivors of this moral electroshock should be plentiful enough, however, for the conversion of the many or the hardening of the few. These are but relative terms for an immeasurable reality. Human frailty or wickedness is such that Satan will have no trouble keeping enough followers for his forthcoming Antichrist.

6) A year after the "Warning" described above, Heaven will work a wonder at Garabandal of such magnitude that it cannot be denied, leaving behind it a permanent and visible sign of what took place. It will also result in the cure of all the lame, the halt and the blind present at that time. Its impact will be such that orthodox Russians will turn to Rome. A similar wonder is announced for Medjugorje.

This "sign," however, which can be recorded on camera and broadcast on television, will not be restricted to Garabandal or Medjugorje. Similar events on a smaller scale are to expected in other spots that have been hallowed by visits of the Virgin.

7) A worldwide economic collapse is foretold.[59] Currency will be abolished: bank cards will prevail. This implies a tighter control of the State over human enterprise: a frightening prospect indeed! Whoever who does not "bear the sign of the beast on his hand or his forehead" will be excluded from business of any kind (*Apoc.* 13, 16-17). To share in social benefits, apostasy will be required under the guise of social conformity.[60] Those who refuse this easy way out will have to grow their own food to escape starvation.

The pattern is clear. National debts in Western Countries are at an all-time high. Since parties dictate policies according to their own interests, the secret of success for politicians resides in providing voters with immediate advantages at the expense of future accountabilities. Once the State is broke, unrest breaks out and revolution ensues. The resulting anarchy leads, as history has shown, either to dictatorship or to foreign intervention. Both should be expected pretty soon in many parts of the world.[61]

---

59 As a result of which, revolutions will occur in such countries as France and Italy. Western Europe, weakened by inner strife, will be invaded by Russia, bolstered by troops from Arab nations, France will be occupied for a year, Paris reduced to rubble, etc..., only to mention the most often foretold disasters.

60 For the heroic souls, the choice will be clear. The merely well-meaning ones will find themselves in a quandary, for a schism will divide the Church. They will have to choose between adjusting their beliefs to the ecumenically-centered Church of the "Beast with two horns," or joining the few social misfits belonging to the persecuted traditional Church. These misfits should be those who refuse the biochip or nanochip through which the devil's minions will exercise subtle collective mind-control.

61 Aloïs Irlmaier, the Bavarian prophet (1894-1959), summarized the evolution of future events concerning his country, and by inference for most of Europe in the following way:

"1) At first, there will be a higher standard of living as never

Rulers on the other hand think in terms of geopolitics. It is not surprising therefore if prophecies announce that China, on its way to world hegemony, will attack the United States while Russia takes simultaneously advantage of a United Europe deprived of American military support. Surprise is the secret of success in modern warfare. Between superpowers, it is the only condition for an eventual victory, as long as nuclear retaliation remains possible.[62]

---

before!

2) As a result will ensue a loss of faith, as never before.

3) As a consequence, there will be a moral perversion, as never before.

4) At this moment, a great number of foreigners will arrive in the country.

5) Inflation will reign. Money will be worth always less and less.

6) Revolution will ensue.

7) And then the Russians will invade [Continental Western Europe] during the night." Upon awakening, the amazed citizen will see them in the streets, just as if this had not been in the cards all along...

62 Surprise has always been the essential strategy of warfare. One nuclear bomb exploding in the North Sea would raise a tsunami of eighty meters high, flooding within minutes London and most of eastern England. As for a nuclear explosion in the stratosphere, it could neutralize the country's electronic communication and electrical distribution systems. Drones of presumably foreign origin have already been spotted hovering over France's nuclear plants, as if these were being mapped out and targeted for future destruction.

8) The Pope will have much to suffer, so will the Church, divided against itself and persecuted both from within and without. The reign of the Antichrist is foretold for three and a half years and with it "the abomination of desolation" *id est*: a sacrilegious Mass.[63] As an actor waiting for his cue in the wings, this impersonator of the Messiah is already present in person today, edging onto the stage on which he will focus the attention of the world.[64] To his success in subverting Christians the False-prophet, or the Beast with two horns mentioned in the Apocalypse (13, 11) will contribute.

This sad state of the Church, which consists essentially in the accommodation of the clergy to the political power, is one of the signs announcing the forthcoming return of Christ, according to Maria Valtorta. At La Salette already, the Virgin had warned that Rome would lose its faith as it becomes the seat of the Antichrist. This means that the majority of the bishops in the world will abandon the following of Christ in favor of that of the "Beast with the horns of a lamb." Thus Manuela of Sievernich, on March 5, 2001, saw in a vision a meeting attended by many cardinals in Italy. "They were discussing the standardization of the Mass without the Eucharist. There will be only a breaking of bread, together with the parishioners, since many do not believe in the Eucharist."[65] This will be what was mentioned

---

63   The sacrilege consisting in the parodic character of its pretense for standing for the "real" Mass.

64   In spite of his deceptiveness, he will be recognizable to readers of Maria Valtorta, for she tells us that "he will be a highly placed person. Not a human star shining in a human heaven, but a luminary in a supernatural sphere," who will have fallen down from grace.

65   As quoted by Paul Josef Jakobus in *Marias grosse Bothschaft an Deutschland und die Welt* (Altötting, Mediatrix-

in Matthew (24, 15): "When ye therefore shall see the abomination of desolation, spoken of by Daniel the prophet, stand in the holy place, who so readeth, let him understand..."

What should we understand, however? Our Holy Mother, in her apparitions at Marpingen (Germany), is very specific on this point: "The churchly freemasonry seeks to destroy the real Church - the one which remains in union with the Pope - through the false ecumenism which accepts all Christian churches." This freemasonry states that each confession has its share of the truth. The avowed purpose of this integration is the removal of the fundament of unity that is the Pope, and a "breaking of Eucharistic bread" of purely symbolic character.[66]

Sister Catherine Filljung (+1915) summarizes thus these dramatic events: "There will be a pontifical election: after the new Pope has been properly elected, the Germans and the Italians will suscitate... an antipope." True Christians "will have no trouble" discriminating between the two.[67]

This schism within the Church embracing at least two-

Verlag, 2010, p.110).

66   Id. pp. 55-57. Such was Maria's warning at Marpingen on June 1, 1989. The idea that the best way to formulate the truth is to compound it from half-truths is a popular fallacy. It is an illusion patterned on the spirit of compromise which democracy furthers on the practical level. Supernatural truth, however, deals with the mysteries of faith which cannot be parceled into disparate elements and then refitted into a whole, as so many parts of a puzzle. A metaphor is not an explanation. The all-too human confusion   resulting from the plurality of views cannot be amended by mediation, however well-meaning this ecumenical attempt may appear to be.

67 See *Prophéties pour la France* by Jean Mathiot (L'Icône de Marie-St Joseph éditeur, Callac de Bretagne, 2008, p. 80).

third of its members should not leave, however, this remaining " small flock" of true believers" unaffected, for they will be the target of a persecution of unparalleled intensity, greater than in the days of Diocletian. Given the modern techniques of supervision they should find it even more difficult to avoid detection than was the case in Soviet Russia. It is to them in particular that the following prophecies apply:

"Now the brother shall betray the brother to death, and the father the son; and children shall arise against their parents; and shall cause them to be put to death. And you shall be hated of all men for my name's sake: but he that shall endure unto the end, the same shall be saved" (Mk 13, 12-14).

Paradoxically, however, we have been told that when this happens, these stalwart souls should rejoice, "look up; and lift up your heads, for your liberation draweth nigh" (Lk 21, 28).

Thus the spirit of tolerance preached by early disciples of *ökuméné* will have led, under the influence of the Antichrist, to its very opposite. And it is likely that Hitler's "final solution" program for the Jews was the devil's blueprint for what Satan had in mind for the true Christians of the XXIst century. In this case, the astonishing spiriting away from this world of elects mentioned in chapter IV (see Mt 24, 40-41 and Lk 17, 34), would amount to Heaven's own program of preservation of future faithful for the thousand year reign of Christ. How those who were not chosen for this mission will be able to account for this vanishing-act of the few is a matter of conjecture. I surmise that they will be puzzled to the point of exasperation.

The Lord told the visionary Luz Amparo of l'Escorial how this would actually happen:

"I, as Son of the Living God, have the power to master

the lightning in my hands and to order my chariots of fire to collect all my elect and transport them in this place, my daughter. Look at these chariots, my daughter, and describe them.

"**Amparo** (while punctuating her description with exclamations of admiration and joy): I see big chariots, with big wheels; inside there are men dressed as lions and eagles, and who always look forward; the wings join each other; they descend. There are millions and millions of eyes around them. Human arms reach out to take the creatures; they land on earth with lions' claws, they carry on their heads diving helmets of sapphire and on their bodies stones of jasper; these wheels are turned towards the four cardinal points. They are... millions..., open their eyes, stretch their arms and choose all these creatures... They are all inside, they close their eyes and open their claws, and their wheels are directed in the same direction..., arrive in another world, another different world; all is splendour and beauty... They all stop, they open anew their eyes, they all begin to leave. Oh, how many are there...! Oh! how beautiful is this place! They will stay there until the Last Judgment... Oh! such greatness!"[68]

The fate of the "creatures" thus chosen, transported "onto the earth of Eden, is reserved to those who have lived the Gospel" (*id.*), explains Christ. And he specifies, so that it be perfectly clear, that this marvelous translation does not concern "the major part of humanity." And, as if by gracious condescendence to our miserable intellectual infirmity, he refers to the text of Matthew (24, 40-41) whose meaning he has just explained, even if the language used, in the naively

---

68 *L'Escorial, Messages, 1992-1998*: Association *Vierge des Douleurs du Pré-Neuf de l'Escorial*, F-64170 Arti, 1999, pp. 44-45, excerpts. Notwithstanding my own interpretation, the way in which the Gospel, the Apocalypse and such visions as those of Luz Amparo relate to each other remains a matter of conjecture.

neo-prophetic and old-testamentary style of Amparo, should, at first, baffle us more than reassure us. But, with these words reminiscent of the Gospel, we are on familiar grounds:

"Some will be taken, others will be left behind; among fathers and sons, some will remain and others will be removed."

Was not Amparo alluding in this vision to these people "having...the name [of the Lamb] and the name of his Father written on their foreheads" whom St John has numbered in the *Apocalypse* as "a hundred and forty-four thousand"? And of whom he says that they "were not defiled by women, for they are virgins" and that they "follow the Lamb wherever he goes"? And he adds: "These were purchased from among men, first-fruits unto God and unto the Lamb... in their mouth there was found no lie; they are without blemish."(14, 1-5).

9) Far from being chastened by experience, **nations will rise up against nations.**[69]

The cue for this event should be the same as for World-War II, but with a difference, warns Julie-Marie Jahenny: "When you see the Aurora Borealis appear, know ye that it is the sign of a forthcoming war. When the light will once more be visible, then will my Mother stand before the setting sun, to warn the good men that the time has come. The wicked, however, will see a frightening monster and will cry out in panic and in despair, but it will be too late. I will save many, many souls."[70]

---

69 Even though the Virgin announced at Medjugorje and Marpingen that there would not be a World War III. Thus the two World Wars we have known could be considered as curtain-raisers for the apocalyptic times. Nonetheless, the invasion of Western Europe by Russian troops with their Arab allies, as announced by Don Bosco and the prophetess of La Fraudaye, has still to take place. Yvonne-Aimée de Malestroit says their occupation of France for one year will be worse than that by the Germans for four years (1940-44). As for the Dresden-like leveling of Paris as a whole, it is, for readers of prophecies, common knowledge.

More precisely, according to Paul Baldauf (*Die dreitätige Finsternis*, Mediatrix, Altötting, 2012, p. 96), "World-War III will be broken off by a darkness of three days," as a catastrophe unrelated to the war itself, but none the less brought about by it, since it will be God's way of bringing the war to an end. "A mighty fire will cleanse the world. This will be Heaven's punishment; which will prevent an endless war. Men would have otherwise made the earth unlivable" - may I suggest, presumably by nuclear contamination. And Paul Baldauf adds paradoxically that "this three day of darkness is a rain of fire and a baptism of fire. Hail and fire = and a third part of the trees was burnt up, and all green grass was burnt up (Apoc. 8, 7) = the first trumpet has sounded."

"And the third angel sounded, and there fell a great star from heaven, burning as it were a lamp, and it fell upon the third part of

Since this monster did not show up during the aurora of Jan. 25-26 1938, it should, on a date yet to come, herald a far worse conflict, at the issue of which many nations will disappear, either by the hand of men, or through natural causes. For our modern civilization is none other than this Babylon whose destruction has been foretold in the *Apocalypse*: "... that great city [that shall] be thrown down, and be found no more," leaving on the sea of time mere ripples of its disappearance (19, 21).

Babylon, best expressed as "the Great Harlot," will be victimized by the circularity of evil (Apoc 17). The theologian Françoise Breynaert suggests that this art of self-destruction will be best promoted by the Antichrist himself who, in this respect, will suffer from the same syndrome as many tyrants whose *hubris* leads them to overreach into disaster the limits of finite capacities. The tower of Babel was built on the premise that since the sky is the limit, progress cannot defeat its own purpose. It should do so, however.

Modern warfare will be a quite extraordinary thing. Once it has reached the level of a direct confrontation between superpowers, whoever initiates it should be aware that he

---

the rivers... And the name of the star is wormwood" (Id. , 10-11).

When the fourth angel sounds his trumpet, the axis of rotation of the earth changes (Id. 12), with the inhabitants of lands in northern temperate climes awakening, in warmer southern latitudes, to a sun rising up in the West. And this is but a small part of the changes to be expected: for instance, the Mediterranean Sea will vanish.

70 As quoted by Claude d'Elendil (*From Nostradamus to Alois Irlmaier*, Domus, 1917 p. 250).

has unleashed the means of his own destruction. Since when, however, have Hitlers stopped playing their own destiny on a fall of dice?

Pending the discovery of a super-weapon such as the laser-ray capable of annihilating a city, here is one of the less-speculative techniques at our disposal: an invisible neutron-polluted line drawn across Germany, presumably by "white" drones, that will kill any living being crossing it, including those shielded in invading tanks. These unmanned vehicles will proceed on blindly, until they run out of fuel (according to Aloïs Irlmaier).

A more plausible version should be that the tanks are unmanned anyway since the next major war will be a war of robots.

10) The prophets of doom announcing ecological disasters will be proved right: it's all in the *Apocalypse* anyway, where we learn what will happen when the seven angels "pour out the seven vials of the wrath of God upon the earth" (16, 1).

For the last three thousand years, men have been warned by Heaven that disaster follows sin as a logical consequence. Few have shown a lasting inclination to learn from past experience. Having sinned upon mountain-tops, Israel was led captive into exile. Decadent Rome was "vandalized" in the days of St. Augustine. Christian nations wasted in religious wars the energies needed for the missionizing of pagan nations. As virtue declines, wars increase. Once religion is outlawed, Gulags are instituted. Legal abortion is social suicide. The acceleration of history multiplies the boomerang effect of immorality; and mankind will soon "self-destruct," if God does not intervene. Unbeknownst from its atheistic *literati*, every upsurge of evil on earth loosens upon us new freshly liberated denizens of hell who have no other purpose in mind than sharing with us, not only in afterlife, but even now as a suitable before-taste, the torments they themselves are afflicted with.

True to tradition, St. John describes what will happen in eschatological terms. Viewing future events from the cause-and-effect perspective of humans, however, such preachers as Father Paul Maria Sigl (Founder of the Congregation of the Children of Mary), adopt a different approach. They claim that it is a mistake to reduce the whiplash effect of immanent justice to God's intervention alone. The bitter taste of the forbidden fruit is that of sin. Breaking the law under the devils' impulse means escaping from God's tutelage. The fire and brimstone falling on Sodom and Gomorrah are the devil's requital for men's failings. For good behavior, God heaps goods upon us; for bad behavior, Satan inflicts evil. And the devil is so eager to respond in kind that he does not always wait for the sinner's death. He is never happier than when he can establish hell on earth, as he did at Auschwitz. He is forever extending his dominion over the living and the dead.

How much Satan must have enjoyed the drowning of sinful mankind under the diluvial waters!

Wartime is fun-time for him. It best expresses his homicidal bent. It is even better in this respect than floods and earthquakes, because in war man is the instrument of his own undoing.

The irony of the situation tickles Satan's sardonic sense of humor. Thus he is at work in both types of disasters. Man's ill-will neutralizes the beneficial interventions of Providence. This is what happened in 18th century France. After the "Philosophes" turned against God, the century of Voltaire and Diderot led to the Revolution and the Napoleonic wars. A mere intellectual rebellion ended in the massacre of millions. When the elite of a nation fosters disbelief in Revelation, the Prince of this World has a free hand.

"As flies to wanton boys are we to the gods,

They kill us for their sport" (Shakespeare).

As these gods of antiquity were none other than demons according to St. Paul, our present-day ideologies are no less pernicious in their impact on our lives. Feminism understood as right-of-life-or-death over the unborn child is Satan's favorite counter to Paul's saying: "woman is saved through childbearing" (I Tim 2, 15). Cutting off prematurely the umbilical cord means breaking her most direct link to salvation. For many of her kind, it was the only one. For the child is God's most precious gift: that of an innocence it can share with its mother.

Whichever way one might choose to interpret the deluge of water in Noah's days, or the rain of fire in those of Lot, as

God's chastisement or the devil's requital, the message is clear: sin does not pay. [71]

If we are to quote the prophetic sources available, however, we find that the forthcoming "three days of darkness" awaiting mankind, which will be a greater disaster than any catastrophe inflicted before or after, shall result from a direct intervention of God, since it will rid the world from its teeming millions of demons along with their human minions. Though this event has been foretold not only by Scriptures but also by countless mystics and saints, its timing is shrouded in mystery. The way it fits in chronologically with the ten other points mentioned in this chapter is a secret which is so well kept that the Father does not share it with the Angels in Heaven, or even with "the Son" (Mc 13, 32). Logically, as the ultimate disaster, it should herald the forthcoming era of peace on earth. Propitiously, it should cut

---

71 This interpretation of Father Sigl is fascinating, since it represents demons as the scavengers of moral decay in this world. They were already known as the avengers of sinfulness in the next world, where they meet out retribution according to deserts. But they had never been presented as eloquently as this as the rapacious vultures preying upon transgressors. Malefactors in person are food for their metaphysical hunger for evil. But what do we then make of the traditional executors of God's will, the good angels? For such is the role they play as instruments of the wrath of God in the *Apocalypse* (15, 1). This is a question which still remains open. Whatever the case, wrongdoing has a boomerang effect. And immanent justice exercises retribution in kind, either now or later. Satan willy-nilly plays his part in this redistribution of evil, since this is the role he assumed when he turned against God. As Prince of this World, he certainly enjoys a greater freedom of action in our times than he ever did before. When men relegate Christ, the Prince of Peace, to the private sphere of the shrinking numbers of true believers, they deliver to the Enemy of mankind the control over their collective conditions of life.

off in its beginnings a World War III whose resort to nuclear weapons would imply the self-destruction of humanity.

This is when eschatological prophecies will have proven to be true by their accomplishment, be it those of the Old Testament, as with Zephania (I, 14-18), or those of the Gospel with Matthew. Since Matthew's text, which is part of Sunday-readings, is common knowledge, let us concentrate on Zephania:

"The great day of the Lord *is* near, *it is* near, and hasteth greatly, *even* the voice of the day of the Lord: the mighty man shall cry there bitterly.

That day *is* a day of wrath, a day of trouble and distress, a day of waste and desolation, a day of darkness and gloominess, a day of clouds and darkness.

A day of the trumpet and alarm against the fenced cities, and against the high towers.

And I will bring distress upon men, that they shall walk like blind men, because they have sinned against the Lord: and their blood shall be poured out as dust, and their flesh as the dung.

Neither their silver nor their gold shall be able to deliver them in the days of the Lord's wrath; but the whole land shall be devoured by the fire of his jealousy[72]: for he shall make a speedy riddance of all them that dwell in the land."[73]

The prophet Zechariah is even more explicit, for he speaks with figures:

---

[72] While Zephaniah describes the "day of the Lord" as the working of "the fire of his jealousy," the modern-day prophets mentioned in this book see it more as the expression of divine Mercy. Is He not saving humanity from itself, as policemen or firemen do when they prevent a madman from jumping from a roof? Left to the devices of the "Prince of the World," humanity would simply "self-destruct."

[73] Zeph. 1:18.

"In the whole land, says the Lord,
two thirds shall be cut off and perish;
and one third shall be left alive.[74]
And I will put this third into the fire,
and refine them as one refines silver,
and test them as gold is tested.
They will call on my name,
and I will answer them" (13, 8-9).[75]

As it is to be expected, non-canonical and more recent prophecies are more explicit, such as those of St. Anna Maria Taigi (1769-1837). After she mentioned that God would "inflict two punishments," the first of which would "come from the earth" and be, so to speak, self-inflicted by humanity, under the guise of "wars, revolutions and other evil," she describes the second as coming "from Heaven":

"Over the whole earth, a deep darkness will reign for three days and three nights. This darkness will make it absolutely impossible to see anything. Furthermore, this darkness will bring with it with a pollution of the air, which will eliminate the enemies of religion, but not exclusively

---

74 With his one third of survivors, Zechariah is more optimistic than the great mystic Saint Mariam Baouardy who witnessed in her visions "terrifying wars savaging all nations; and she used to say that when the wars would be over and following the 'three days of darkness', pestilential darkness during which men who are addicted to vice will perish, so that only one quarter of mankind would survive, all the rest having died in the fray" (As quoted in *Chrétiens Magazine* of February 2017, p. 12).

75 According to Iannuzzi, this will be "a Particular Judgment." And he quotes the stigmatic Therese Neumann: "Our Lord himself called it a minor judgment." For St. John Vianney: "It will be like a sign of the last judgment." (See: *Antichrist and the Antichrist and the End Times*, pp.68-69). It will be different, however, insofar as it will not address "the living and the dead" but only the living.

these. As long as the darkness lasts, it will be impossible to have light. Blessed candles alone can be lit and bring light. He who during the darkness opens out of curiosity a window and looks outside, or leaves the house, will immediately fall dead.[76] During these three days, people should remain at home, pray the rosary and beg God for mercy—all windows shuttered or covered with newspapers. The sight of hell at work is more than flesh can bear and stay alive. During this darkness, all the known and hidden enemies of the Church will be destroyed. Only a few, whom God wants to convert, will stay alive."[77]

Thus a trial by fire, from an exploding heavenly body,[78]

Furthermore, it will be both individually and collectively selective with its eradication of whoever is in a state of mortal sin, while, in its upheaval of the elements, it will insure either the survival, or partial or total destruction of nations according to their past and recent history. Thus not only will populations be affected but the general topography of the land they live in, which could shrink or increase in direct proportion to their cumulative misbehavior or accumulated virtue. In other words, this parousia will be "the Judgment of Nations." The "parable of talents" will apply on a geographical scale. Of Great Britain, for instance, little will remain – but this is my personal intuition - while a new land will surge up in the Atlantic, as if it were a rebirth of Atlantis.

76 Presumably because no one can survive the sight of hell, such as it is, or of its denizens such as they are, without falling dead. And when all hell is loosed on earth, then woe unto them who think they can glimpse at it without hurt and survive the shock! Absolute evil is more than mere flesh and blood can bear.

77 As quoted by Paul Baldauf: *Die dreitätige Finsternis* (Mediatrix-Verlag, Altötting; pp. 94-95). On p. 96, he lists the names of 26 prophets of modern times who announce and describe the three days of darkness, among which are Padre Pio, Marie-Julie Jahenny, Brigit of Sweden, and Katharina Emmerich.

78 Conchita, the visionary of Garabandal, likes to point out

should reduce selectively, and by two thirds or more, the population of this world. "Selectively" means that the angels will "separate the wheat from the tares." Thus, the "great tribulation" announced by Matthew will spare most of those humans who are in the state of grace. It will furthermore not affect those who have been "removed" beforehand by angels, according to Luke, when "of two men in the field, one shall be taken and the other left behind" (17,36). This is consonant with Paul's statement that "All shall not die, but all will be transformed" (I Cor 15, 51).

For those of our readers who like to think in terms of natural disasters even when those catastrophes are of supernatural origin, the nature of the impending destructive chaos on earth can be readily imagined in a few words. This is what Luz Amparo of El Escorial has to say:

"I have seen huge asteroids of several kilometers that men have not yet discovered which are on their way towards earth... Let me repeat it, I have seen almost ten thousand asteroids, as yet unnamed, but which are falling down towards [our] earth."[79]

---

the hypothetical character of this chastisement of humanity, even though she is personally convinced that, considering mankind's constantly expanding sinfulness, it has become inescapable. "Anyway; *I have seen* it. Yes, I can affirm that, if it takes place, it will be worse than if we were encircled by fire, worse than if we had the fire above us and below us. I do not know how much time there will be between the *Warning* and the chastisement" (As quoted by Anna-Maria Turi in *Pourquoi la Vierge apparaît aujourd'hui* (Félin, Paris, 1988, p. 238).

79 *Catéchèse à l'Escorial* (Rassemblement à son Image, Capelle, Ohnet le Château, 2013, p. 138). If the dinosaurs disappeared because a heavenly body hit the peninsula of Yucatan 150 million years ago, what will be the fate of mankind, when so many asteroids fall like a rain of fire upon the earth?

These are "the stars of the sky [falling] to the earth," mentioned in the Apocalypse (6, 13), "as the fig tree sheds its winter fruit when shaken by a gale."

Seen in perspective, the promise of forthcoming wonders outweighs the warning of oncoming disasters. I am not sure, of course, that these fearful events will follow sequentially as I have shown above. I am merely highlighting what is already well known. This phase of transition, full of trials and overshadowed by disasters, between the reign of Satan and that of Christ, could be brief enough to last one generation. The better to survive, with our own soul unscathed, from the consequences of the wars within and without and the perils inflicted by a disintegrating nature, the Virgin offers us refuge within the protective folds of her cloak.

11) The apostles' mistake, when Christ, again and again, announced that he would die a violent death and then resuscitate, is that they focused on what they thought was the implausibility of the warning and forgot about the resurrection. Humanity will be going through a somewhat similar process of death and revival. Since it does not listen to the prophecies concerning the impending "judgment of nations," it disbelieves even more those concerning the renewal of all things. If "all the world is a theater," a dress rehearsal of the "Final Judgment" seems appropriate. And the lessons to be learned from such an experience, will benefit the world for a millennium. When death is the price for sin, life is the reward for virtue. For once in history, virtue will bring more than its own reward,[80] not only in next life but also in this one, and furthermore on a collective level. This smaller, but better part of mankind that will survive the Apocalypse, will be like Job after he was tried by Satan: "the Lord blessed the latter end of Job more than his beginning" (Jb 42, 12). For it shall come to them who do the Will of God in the privileged status which is now theirs, that the words of the Gospel will apply with increased effectiveness. Thus it is quite literally that **they shall receive during this life "a hundredfold" for what they did for the Kingdom of God**, and very much more than that in the life hereafter:

"There is no man that hath left house, or brethren, or sisters, or father, or mother, or wife, or children, or lands, for my sake, and the gospel's;

But that he shall receive an hundredfold now in this time, houses, and brethren, and sisters, and mothers, and children, and lands, with persecutions; and in the world to come eternal life." (Mc 10, 29-30) .

In Marc's enumeration, the only word that does not

---

80 Or twice in the history of mankind, considering the Deluge.

apply fully to the time to come, is the word "persecutions," since this would entail an active participation of the devil who will by then have been locked up in hell for a "thousand years." "The time to come," this millennium of God's reign, is indeed a return to a happier state, which had already been intimated in many respects in Adam's paradise. There are differences, of course, since Satan, for a seemingly long while, has been relegated to hell. On the one hand, it seems doubtful men will enjoy as sovereign an estate as their forefather Adam did. On the other, God's direct intervention should preclude a mere return to what has already been. According to the descriptions of Isaiah, Ezekiel and Zechariah, however, the causal link between performance and reward on earth should regain somewhat of its pristine integrity. Christ made us aware that justice is an investment in a treasure in heaven. In the Old Testament, justice had been shown as an assurance of happiness on earth. Though Job was tried by the loss of all his goods, he deserved a better fate, as he himself found out in the end. Abraham, by his willingness to sacrifice his only son, reaped an almost unlimited progeny. And David was victorious as long as he was virtuous. Thus, tomorrow, with the return of Christ, the ethical logic of the Old Testament will be reconciled with that of the New. For the logic of love transcends that of justice, but does not revoke it. Not an iota of the Scripture shall be canceled. And the apparent opposition between a saying such as "My Kingdom is not of this world" and the accomplishment of the request of Christ in the Our Father, "Thy Kingdom come," will at last have been overcome.

12) We know what diversity of events to expect between the present times and the Great Tribulation, such as a Warning from Heaven, a Wonder for many to see, a world-wide economic recession and ensuing state-control, further-more wars of fearsome magnitude, and lastly persecutions of the Church followed by its virtual demise under the usurped authority of the Antichrist...

What we do not know, however, is how to fit, amidst this tragic process, an event no less astonishing because it has been announced for so many centuries that it seems to have grown stale through repetition: that is **the forthcoming reign of "the Great Monarch,"** a descendant of St. Louis who will be his equal in piety, and yet whose military exploits will outshine those of Charlemagne. He will extend the boundaries of his kingdom beyond those of Europe unto the shores of the Jordan, bringing with it peace and prosperity, for the span of his long reign...

The contrast between black and white could not be more sharply defined than between the previous eschatology of disaster and this promise of forthcoming renewal. The dividing line can only be those three days of darkness, which we have already described, when Satan and his earthly minions will be precipitated to hell by Michael and his angels. The difficulty we encounter at this point is that a military campaign, however justified and successful, hardly seems congenial with the era of peace and brotherhood announced by the prophecies for Paul VI's "civilization of love"...

An analogy might be of help. The mission of this Bourbon offshoot will be as providential and as astonishing as that of Joan of Arc. She led the armies of the French Dauphin to victory against all odds until his crowning at Rheims. At which point her calling paralleled that of Christ at his Passion, and she was treacherously delivered to her enemies who burned her at the stake. In this world of ours ruled by Satan, martyrdom is the natural price for supernaturally induced achievements. But once the Evil One and his cohorts have been banned from our earth, divine dynamics embodied in saints will no longer be diverted from their initial purpose by devilish interference. It must be supposed, therefore, that after his unexplainable early military successes, our new French Joan of Arc will see his opponents crushed by direct heavenly intervention during the "three nights of darkness." This should open the way for a triumphal and unopposed march to the East, such of which medieval Crusaders could only have dreamt.

We know, however, that the timing of this trial by heavenly fire is a well-kept secret. What is significant in the prophecies concerning "the Great Monarch," however, is that they reveal that each nation has a providential calling, no less highly personalized than that proper to each individual. Before God, men have a mission to fulfill, whether singly or collectively. That of France was formulated fifteen hundred centuries ago by pope Athanasius II in his letter to Clovis when he called this country "the first-born daughter of the Church." On the night of Christmas when that monarch was baptized at Rheims with three thousand of his men, the ministering bishop St. Remi made the following speech:

"Learn, my son, that the kingdom of France is pre-destined by God for the defense of the Roman Church... This kingdom shall be one day great among all nations. And it will extend to the boundaries of the Roman empire. And it will submit all people to its scepter. It will endure until the end of time. It shall be victorious and prosperous as long as it is faithful to the Roman Faith. But it will be severely chastised whenever it is unfaithful to its vocation. Towards the end of times, a descendant of the French kings will reign over all of the Roman empire of old. He will be the greatest of the Kings of France and the last of his race. After a more than glorious reign, he will go to Jerusalem on the Mount of Olives to depose his crown and his scepter. Thus will come to an end the Holy and Christian Empire."[81]

Is it possible that St. Rémi took his cue, from the following prophecy of St. Augustine's, who around 400 wrote that "some of our doctors say that a King of the Franks, who will come in the last times of the world, will rule over the Roman Empire."

An almost always overlooked detail in Joan of Arc's brief and providential career is her initial request to the Dauphin, as condition for any future help from Heaven, that he divest himself of his own Kingly birthright over France and hand it over to Christ. Against all human expectation, this all too weakly Prince - but what did he have to lose? - turned over his Kingdom in an official act duly notarized. This done, Joan took command of the army and flew from victory to victory until Charles VII was crowned at Rheims. In the same spirit, St. Francis of Paule (1416-1507) assured Louis XI, his penitent, that a descendant of his would be "as the sun among the stars":

"In the whole universe, there will only be one Holy Father and a great king" whose empire "will last until the end of times."

The Venerable Barthelemy Holzhauser (1615-1658), who ministered in Bingen (Germany) announced an era when "all the nations will share the one and only Catholic Faith" under

---

81 This quotation and those which will follow proceed from Jean Mathiot's "Prophéties pour la France" (Ed. 'L'Icône de Marie - St Joseph, Callac de Betagne, 2008); my translation.

the dominion of the "Great Monarch" who was foreseen by the apostle John:

"And I saw and behold, a white cloud, and upon the cloud sitting like to a son of man, having upon his head a crown of gold and in his hand a sharp sickle... And he who sat on the cloud cast his sickle upon the earth, and the earth was reaped" (Apoc 14, 14-16).

Of course, this is Christ himself. Yet between Him and the human kingship of his choice, there is a necessary bond. After this cryptic vision, what the Curé d'Ars has to say in 1830 sounds more matter-of-fact:

"After the destruction of Paris shall appear the monarch who will reestablish all things... Religion will flower as never before."

Mélanie Calvat, the visionary of La Salette (1848-1894), solves the question of chronology when she sets "the great pope and the great monarch" definitively after the "awful, terrible and general tribulation..." She also seems to put a damper on the literal interpretation of St. John who saw Satan confined to hell for no less than "one thousand years." For though men will at first "live in the fear of God..." said Mélanie, "25 years of bountiful harvests will make them forget" that their sins "are the cause of all afflictions on earth."[82]

Marie-Julie Jahenny of Blain foretells in 1905 of a "hidden king" who will come when the crisis is at its worst,

---

82 With this very short version of a "civilization of love" on earth, she casts a hypothetical character on the optimistic speculations of our previous chapters. But let us not forget that "prophecy," according to the expression of Father Laurentin, should never be understood "as history before history." Past events cannot be undone while most future ones, however foreseeable they may be, cannot but share the undetermined character of human liberty to which they are related.

since he will bring it to an end"... To him, God will "inspire the knowledge of the necessary means for the regeneration of humanity, such as God wills it."

To Marcel Vian, Vietnamese mystic and martyr (1928-1959), our Lord revealed what were his plans: "I will use France for the universal extension of my Love." And to St. Mariam of Bethléhem (1846-1878): "Soon will France triumph and be the Queen [of Kingdoms]." "It will even govern Syria."[83]

The four horsemen of the Apocalypse (6, 1-8), Albrecht Dürer

---

83 As quoted in *Chrétiens Magazine* of Feb. 2017, p. 13.

XII

WHAT ABOUT THE JEWS?

"Ye shall not see me, until the time come when ye shall say; 'Blessed is he that cometh in the name of the Lord'" (Lk 13, 35).

At this point we are faced by the most difficult problem of all, by what the French call "La Question juive." This People is an enigma. And the riddle which stands before us is: "When will this people claim through conversion its full brotherhood with Christ? When will it stop asking: 'When will the Messiah come?' and answer its own question with the following one: 'When shall we come to Him?'"

For the standard answer is the one which Pope Benedict offers in a recent book: "Since the first shall be the last, the Jewish people will be the last to convert, and therefore this will happen at the end of history" (my summary).

Let us not forget that there are two kinds of Jews. In this respect, they are not different from the Gentiles. There are those who practice their religion, and there are those who have no religion at all even if they consider themselves genetically or culturally Jewish. Today these cultural Jews are at least three times more numerous, but since outside of Israel 50 % of them are marrying Gentiles, their distinctiveness may disappear with time. Whatever the case, most of the prophecies we are concerned with were formulated in the days of St. Paul, when the option was between becoming a Christian or remaining a Jew, even if, at first, in practice the dividing line was often difficult to perceive or to establish.

Christ had already prophesied: "Jerusalem will be trampled by the Gentiles, until the times of the Gentiles are fulfilled" (Lk 21, 24). Now, the "times of the Gentiles" will be fulfilled, when two conditions are realized:

1) the Gospel has been preached to the whole world;

2) an almost general apostasy has taken place.

These conditions are contradictory. How can they be reconciled? The only way that this is possible is by mentioning that number one precedes number two chronologically, just as the day precedes the night that follows it... To be able to apostasy, one must first have been a believer. We have witnessed this process with our own eyes when within a single generation in Europe, practicing Catholics or Christians have become minorities. Thus Christ could say:

1) "When the Son of man comes, will he find faith on earth?" (Lk 18, 8).
2) "And this gospel of the kingdom will be preached throughout the whole world, as a testimony to all nations, and then the end will come" (Mt 24, 14).

For the Son of man will not come once, but twice.

And St. Paul warns us that this Coming, whenever it may be, will be preceded by a brief reign of the Antechrist, whomever he may also be. For there are many Antichrists, but only two fully worthy of bearing that name: the first, by his intimate and privileged connection with the devil, and the second, because he will be the devil himself.

"[The Lord] will not come, unless the rebellion [apostasia] comes first, and the man of lawlessness is revealed, the son of perdition, who opposes and exalts himself against every so-called god or object of worship, so that he takes his seat in the temple of God, proclaiming himself to be God" (2 Thes 2; 2-5).[84]

This proclamation of divinity on the part of the Antichrist seems to point to Antichrist number 2, in other words to the Devil himself, and not to Antichrist number 1 who is the "Beast with two Horns like a Lamb" (Apoc 13, 11) who will appear immediately before the First Return of Christ. But this is not a decisive argument, since this spurious Lamb does look suspiciously like a Pseudo-Messiah himself.

Whatever the case, there is a magnificent passage in Zechariah (12, 10), where the Old Testament seems to confirm explicitly the New Testament, in which Christ says, as he is about to die: "O Jerusalem, Jerusalem... I tell you, you will not see me again until you say: 'Blessed is he who comes in the name of the Lord'" (Mt 23, 39).

For they will see Him, says Zechariah, as the one they have pierced:

---

84 This obsession on the part of Lucifer to unseat God in the eyes of men, after he failed to do so in person in the sight of angels, thanks to Michael's intervention, is the constitutive part of his sinful make-up. Eternity is, in moral terms, a prolongation of time, and in this short spell before history stops short, the Evil One will attempt to receive from mere creatures of flesh and blood the worship due to God alone. Had he not, supreme irony, already tried to seduce the Man-God himself into recognizing this claim: "If thou wilt worship before me, the whole world shall be thine" (Mt 4,9)? What he failed to obtain from Christ in the desert, he bargains he will have no trouble to obtain, at the end-times, from most of the rest of humanity. But his success shall then be as short-lived as it is delusive.

"And I will pour out on the house of David and the inhabitants of Jerusalem a spirit of compassion and supplication, so that, when they look on him whom they have pierced, they shall mourn for him, as one mourns for an only child, and weep bitterly over him, as one weeps over a firstborn" (12, 10).

And this is where Dr. Feingold, a Jewish convert, after bringing the previous biblical passages to our attention, quotes Cardinal Journet:

"There will be a day when the Israel of the flesh will again be one with the Israel of the spirit - the great ingathering which the Apostle says will be like 'life from the dead' (Rm 11-15)."[85]

For if the "failure" of the Jews "means riches for the Gentiles, how much more will their full inclusion mean!" (Rm 11, 12).

"[While] if their rejection means the reconciliation of the world, what will their acceptance mean but life from the dead?" (Rm 11, 15).

St. Thomas Aquinas believes that "the Jews [will be received] again by God" at the very moment when "the Gentile faithful [have grown] cold, according to Matthew 24,12:

"And because wickedness is multiplied, most men's love will grow cold."

Thus "those also who completely fall - deceived by the Antichrist - will be *restored to their pristine fervor by the converted Jews.* And thus, as through the fall of the Jews the Gentiles were reconciled after being enemies, so after the

---

85 See Dr. Lawrence Feingold: "The Conversion of Israel and the Second Coming" in *The Hebrew Catholic* (St Louis, Winter 2010-2011, p. 23). His article was an inspiration for me and I follow him closely, except in matters of chronology.

conversion of the Jews, the end of the world being imminent, there will be the general resurrection, through which men will go from death to immortal life."[86]

According to Thomas Aquinas, therefore, it is the conversion of the Jews that signalizes, for our general benefit and instruction, that "the end of the world is imminent." This is very practical, since their conversion shall be for us a warning that we had better convert too. And we should have very little time to do so. Better late than never! To see the end of the world as a logical sequel to the Christianization of Israel, presents the advantage that it illustrates literally the words which Christ applies implicitly to his fellow-Jews in the parable "of the day laborers": "The first will be the last," the expression "the last" being taken fully and literally.

Since Thomas Aquinas did not believe that there would be an intermediate return of Christ as distinct and separate from his last and ultimate return, he had no other choice. His standpoint is also that of Benedict XVI, in opposition to Saint Bonaventure's thesis that an intermediate return of Christ should indeed be expected. In which case, of course, the conversion of the Jews occurring at the time of Antichrist number one, would allow as a consequence these Jews to fulfill belatedly and ultimately their initial vocation, which had been to supply the nascent Church with zealous missionaries. At first only a small remnant of them had been willing to do so. And thus St. Paul could place the Jews and the Gentiles in dialectical opposition. Since their loss had been our gain, he claims our loss should be their gain. By the word "loss" he means the "loss of faith." For the prophecy of Christ applies quite as fittingly both to his first and to his last

86 Commentary on Rom 11, 15, in *Super epistolas S. Pauli lectura*, ed. Raphael Cai (Turin, Marietti, 1953), I:166, n. 890, as quoted by Dr. Feingold.

return:

"When the Son of Man returns, will he still find faith on earth?" (Lk 18, 8). Thus the Jews might have, just as well, a decisive role to play in each case, since "their acceptance will signify life from the dead" for the rest of the world (Rm 11, 15). "Life from the dead!" What a powerful expression! For it means that the "rest of the world," having fallen from grace, will be evangelized a second time by Jews, but this time not by a mere handful of apostles and disciples. In this perspective, how understandable becomes the hatred of the godless towards them, beginning with Voltaire, Proudhon, Karl Marx and culminating with Hitler!

It seems as if we could choose to set the conversion of the Jews in the near or the distant future according to conjecture. We can even imagine a scenario in which a sizable amount of them convert pretty soon, while a no less important amount of them await until the millennium is over to do so, circa 3000 AD.

Cardinal Journet, however, expresses what I consider the most optimistic and plausible version of things to come in the following terms:

"[One may] assume that Israel's return will take place within the very web of historic time, that indeed it is meant to influence the course of the centuries to come after it..."

And he explains this with the argument that "Israel's entry [should] provoke within the Church such a resurgence of love as could be compared to a return of the dead to life."[87]

---

87 Charles Cardinal Journet, "The Mysterious Destinies of Israel," *The Bridge: A Yearbook of Judaeo-Christian Studies*; ed. John Osterreicher, vol 2 (New York: Pantheon Books, 1956), 84-85. As mentioned by Dr. Feingold who quotes Cardinal Journet as if to uphold his own end-of-the-world opinion, which the cardinal shares, while considering the opposite point of view as plausible in

In other words, the conversion of the Jews would be the signal of this "civilization of love" announced by Paul VI, which will flower during the millennium as the crowning glory of the Church of Philadelphia.

Now the Church of Philadelphia, according to the computation of theologians, is about to be our Church. We are the ones who are intimately concerned: we, and even more appropriately, our brethren in Monotheism. For John, from his exile of Patmos, quotes the forceful terms which Christ addresses to the Angel of the Church of our times:

"Behold, I will make them of the synagogue of Satan, which say they are Jews, and are not, but do lie; behold, I will make them to come and worship before thy feet, and to know that I have loved thee" (Ap 3, 9).

Harsh as these words are, they are chronologically important, because they signify, in literal terms, that those very Jews who unbeknownst belong, because of their stubbornness, to the party of Satan, should pretty soon convert *en masse* to our Church: this very Church whose present state of dereliction hardly seems to justify such a favorable outcome. As for the precise circumstances of this prodigious homecoming, we will have to rely on other prophetical texts.

This is today a minority opinion, however, since it corresponds logically to an option which is only available to those theologians who believe in the Intermediate Return of Christ.

How admirable are the ways of the Lord! This Jewish nation, the most prophetic of all because of its history, has been preserved against all odds as a spiritual entity because of an initial choice of God and for the completion of the role that it has also been chosen to fulfill in the end times. Its

---

its own right.

persecution by evil forces, and most recently again, testifies that the devil is fully aware that the Jews present for himself and his reign a definite threat. Since he is a reader of the Bible too, the Holocaust was his ultimate attempt to counter the fulfillment of God's plan. He too shares obviously with me the opinion that the conversion of the Jews is for pretty soon. Can I claim him as an authority on the subject? What a paradox!

For that conversion to take place, however, something extraordinary has to happen, something no less unexpected than the return of Elias and Henoch, such as it is described by John in the Apocalypse. Now, tradition has it that the persona which John the Baptist evoked at first for the Jews is the very one who will prepare the return of Christ, namely Elias. As for Henoch, he symbolizes laymen, while Elias stands for the Priesthood. They are customarily identified with "the two Anointed who stand before the Lord" (Zech. 4,14). Therefore, less plausible than Henoch, as future apostles of the Jews, is Moses, their previous leader to the Holy Land, present with Elias at the Transfiguration of Christ.

John describes the full might of the world led by the Antichrist exercising its enmity to the Church in a persecution lasting 42 months. This is what "the Voice from Heaven" has to say:

"And I will give power unto my two witnesses, and they shall prophesy a thousand two hundred and threescore days, clothed in sackcloth.

These are the two olive trees, and the two candlesticks standing before the God of the earth.

And if any man will hurt them, fire proceedeth out of their mouth, and devoureth their enemies: and if any man will hurt them, he must in this manner be killed.

These have power to shut heaven, that it rains not in the days of their prophecy: and have power over waters to turn them to blood, and to smite the earth with all plagues as often as they will" (Apoc 11, 3-6, RSV).

These two witnesses will thus exercise a power unheard of on earth since Elias was borne up to heaven in a chariot of fire. But he who could stand up to kings in his heyday will be no match to the power of darkness then engulfing the world:

"And when they shall have finished their testimony, the beast that ascendeth out of the bottomless pit shall make war against them, and shall overcome them and kill them.

And their dead bodies shall lie in the street of the great city, which spiritually is called Sodom and Egypt, where also our Lord was crucified.

And they of the people and kindred and tongues and nations shall see their dead bodies three days and a half; and shall not suffer their dead bodies to be put in graves.

And they that dwell upon the earth shall rejoice over them; and make merry...; because these two prophets tormented that dwelt on the earth.

And after three days and an half the Spirit of life from God entered into them, and they stood upon their feet; and great fear fell upon them which saw them.

And they heard a great voice from heaven saying unto them, Come up hither.

And they ascended up to heaven in a cloud; and their enemies beheld them.

And the same hour was there a great earthquake, and the tenth part of the city fell,

And in the earthquake were slain of men seven thousand: and the remnant were affrighted, and gave glory to the God of heaven" (Apoc 11, 7-13, RSV).

And well they might! For this resurrection of the "two

witnesses" will prove the undoing of the prestige of the Antichrist in the eyes of the Jews, announcing his forthcoming fall and bringing about their conversion.

Once again, this extraordinary occurrence could be read either as pertaining to the end of time which is the end of the world, or more convincingly still to the end of times, which is for pretty soon. I leave it up to the reader![88]

Let him consult on this point *Apocalypse* 3, 8, as we do in our Addendum, and rely on the prophetic words of Jesus when his Passion was about to begin:

> "And Jerusalem will be trodden down by the Gentiles, until the times of the nations be fulfilled" (Lk 21, 24).

Now that Jerusalem is no longer "trodden down by the Gentiles," "the times of the nations is fulfilled," or in other words "the times of the Gentiles is coming to an end" with that of the Nations they belong to. It is not the end of time that is close by, but the end of times, i.e., that end of history such as we know it, as made of separate and conflicting nations, and not of one Kingdom.

> "The glory of this latter house shall be greater than that of the former, saith the Lord of hosts: and in this place will I give peace..." (Haggai 2, 9).

Such indeed is the promise of the fulfillment of prophecies concerning the Holy Town, recently recognized by President Trump as the capital of the State of Israel. For me, the

---

[88] See *L'Evangile tel au'il m'a été révélé* (Centro Editoriale Valtortiano, Isola de Liri, Italy. Tome 10, p. 453)

most convincing prediction is the one to be found in Maria Valtorta's mystically inspired "Life of Christ":

"As announced by the prophets, it is here at Jerusalem where the King-Messiah has been anointed and acclaimed and from which He has risen that His reign in the world must start, and it is here again where the Synagogue, because of its all too horrible crimes, has received from God a label of repudiation that the New Temple must rise, towards which all the nations will flock.

Consult the prophets: they have said it all. My Mother at first, and then the Spirit Paraclete, will make you understand the words of the prophets concerning this [generation].

Need I point out the providential role played in our days by those multiple Marian apparitions, from Fatima to Medjugorje, whose implicit or even explicit message is that te Day of the Lord is neigh: a message which has mostly been obfuscated by churchmen...Have we not been told, however, that the return of Christ would be as unexpected as was the Deluge or the break-in of the robber at night? Neither heaven nor hell give notice of their impending proximity.

Even though our Babylon is doomed, nothing can prevail ultimately against the Church. Should a geographic displacement of the hub of Christianity in favor of the City of David signal its spiritual renewal as the ultimate accomplishment of the City of God on earth?

This would mean the fulfillment of the following prophecy:

"In those days, ten men of every nation, speaking in different tongues, shall take hold, yes, take hold of every Jew by the edge of his garment and say, "Let us go with you, for we have heard that God is with you." (Zechariah 8, 23).

"And the stars of the sky fell to the earth as the fig tree sheds its winter fruit when shaken by a gale…" (Apoc 6, 13), Albrecht Dürer

XIII

AND WHAT ABOUT THE MOSLEMS?

They represent now the greatest threat to the Evangelization of the world, pre-empting perhaps both other competing entities for this destructive role: the Beast which comes from the Sea which stands for Freemasonry, and the Beast with the ten heads, "one of which was miraculously cured." This last head signifies Communism, if not in its early Stalinist form, at least metamorphosed into a more certain conformity to liberal economy.

Who indeed at this time is responsible for the most effective persecutions of Christians, if not the followers of Mohammed? They have taken over this bloody task from the Communists, whose present regimes are comparatively more accommodating towards Christians than those of the preceding generations.

The threat of a general Islamization of Europe is implemented by those migrants from the Middle East and Africa. As a kind of requital for past colonization, they are, by their higher birthrate, readying a political or even possibly a violent takeover of their host nations.

Statistics and commonsense agree with this pattern which reflects what happened in previous centuries when Islam spread from the Middle-East to Northern Africa and parts of Europe.

If the lessons of the past are not obvious enough, however, to let us know what our future will be, we can rely on such a prophet as Marie-Jeanne Jahenny.

This visionary and mystic used the expression: "La France deviendra mahomète, niant la divinité du Christ" ("France will be Moslem, negating the divinity of Christ") to summarize the takeover she describes in great detail.

After the financial crash, which will affect more especially the socially dependent classes in the suburbs of Paris peopled by North Africans and Middle-easterners, this culturally alien milieu, according to Jahenny, will rise up in revolt and set the Bourgeois town center on fire. Chastened into submission by this catastrophe, the left-oriented government will share power with this wave of the future whose ascendancy it unwittingly promoted; and since there is a momentum in success, some Catholic priests and prelates will rally to the new religion.[89]

There is nothing democratic about revolution. It is always fomented by a minority, even when it masquerades as the majority, nor is there anything republican about Islam, although the latter could end up controlling parts of Europe within 30 to 40 years through sheer weight of numbers.

Revolution and devastation brought about by a similar constellation of causes are foreseen for other European countries, almost as a domino-effect, such as in Italy. This country will be vandalized by iconoclasts and Rome will not be spared. The Pope will have to "flee [from the Vatican], only to return after two hundred days."[90]

---

89 On Jahenny, see Claude d'Elendil: *De Nostradamus à Alois Irlmaier*, Domus, 2017, p.175.

90 According to the Franciscan nun Erna Stieglitz from Augsburg (1894-1975): Id. p. 176).

Powerful as it may be, Islam is blighted by its very nature as a heresy compounded out of two Monotheisms, the Jewish and the Christian one, without benefiting from the active tutelage of God. As a "Religion of the Book," it is as divisive as Protestantism, with additional tribal violence. Its intolerance is registered in its very constitution. It treats Christianism as a plague, and frightens would-be converts with the death-penalty.

Did Christ have Islam in mind when he warned that a time would come when "the brother will deliver up his brother to death, and the father his child..." (Mark 13, 12)? It shall be that " many will betray one another and hate one another" (Mt 24, 10). Hatred is the spice of life for Jihadists. Converts from Islam are targeted with a fatwa, irrespective of family ties.

This aberrant religion could destroy in Europe the visible cultural heritage of two thousand years of Christianity.

When virtue loses its moorings, Humanitarianism is defenseless: it invites those who deny it to shelter and dwell under its protective folds.

The triumph of Islam should be brief however: its warlike momentum will crest and waste in the turmoil it creates, while a weakened and disorganized Europe offers Russia that power vacuum which will allow Putin or his follower to carry out their hegemonic project.[91]

---

91 The seer Alois Irlmaier, with a sense of humor, describes their initial success in terms reminiscent of the surprise takeover of Crimea by Putin, even if this time it should be less discreet. Late bar-hoppers will be surprised on their way home by Russian tanks, and stolid citizen, aroused from their sleep, will rub their eyes in amazement at dawn at the sight of foreign uniforms in the streets. In all the electric plants of Western Europe, fossil-fueled or nuclear, the power transmission facilities will have been selectively bombed out. Today already drones of an unknown

Will the USA risk retaliation by coming to the rescue of its ally? Probably not, since they themselves will be then under siege from China's almost inexhaustible armies.

Might is not limitless however, and the just retribution of hubris comes from unexpected quarters. When all seems lost, Heaven will intervene with the forthcoming "Great Monarch" as mentioned in our Chapter 11, section 12.

And we know from countless prophecies that Russia at long last will overcome its anti-Roman bias and join the Catholic fold, as a result of the Great Miracle announced at Garabandal. One can assume that the Russian army will have found by then its way into Spain.

Another wonder at a later date will be the a change of hearts among the descendants of Ismaël, according to Saint Grignion de Montfort: "[Mary] will extend the Kingdom of Christ over idolaters and Muslims," as already mentioned in our chapter IX. Had she not already revealed this intent,

---

origin are observed hovering above Felsenheim and other power units as if mapping out future targets. The ensuing blackout, according to prophetess Yvonne-Aimé of Malestroit, should last for a year. Furthermore, France occupied both by a foreign army and Moslem militias, will suffer then more damage than the Nazis had inflicted. A refuge has been provided, however, for the inhabitants of the section of land situated west of a line going from Le Havre to Bordeaux. As for those readers whose sense of inherent justice is acute, let them be reassured: none of the invaders from the East will survive their initial success. Irlmaier sees flocks of white birds (American drones?) depositing an invisible trail of radioactive substance upwards from Prague to the sea which no living creatures can cross without perishing: driverless tanks will pursue their route until they run out of fuel. Ye humans beware! Modern warfare will be technological to the point where robots take over. And Russia, having lost its weaponry in its attempt to take over Western Europe, may then be threatened in turn from elsewhere.

when she began appearing over Coptic Churches, at Zeitoun or elsewhere in Egypt, beginning in 1988, to the amazement of Moslem crowds of up to 250 000?

The opening of the seventh seal with the falling of the star named Wormwood and the angel saying, "Woe, woe, woe to the inhabitants of the earth!" (Apoc 8-9, 3), Albrecht Dürer

XIV

THE END TIMES

"In the end is my beginning," for the finality of an act determines its nature. History, in its unfolding, reveals its meaning with greater clarity, as it approaches consummation. Thus, it is an intellectual and spiritual privilege to live as we do in the "end times," even if this proves at first hard to bear. While men are savaging each other, and the world is unhinged from its moorings, we can still rejoice at the thought that "our deliverance is near."

Thus, let us bear with patience those among us who remain blind to the "signs of the times." "Ils se crèvent agréablement les yeux" is the usual French expression. "they enjoy gouging their eyes out," at least those of their soul. For the evidence supplied by events is overwhelming. Never, since the days of Christ, has Heaven expressed as openly and forcibly its intention to intervene in the affairs of men.

There was the warning given at La Salette (1846) which seems to us in retrospect somewhat removed from its object. Through the mouthpiece of its visionary, Mélanie Calvat, it castigated the worldliness of the clergy in terms more appropriate to our own epoch than it did then. For if priests and bishops enjoyed in the nineteenth century a higher social status, they were also far more open to supernatural manifestations. Today however, what is both unexplainable in scientific terms, and is yet as real as what can be measurable, is not accepted as evidence before the court of public opinion. And so many dignitaries of our Church pay obeisance to this commonly shared bias, to the point that obvious charismatas are overlooked as being irrelevant. The prejudice against religion, which Pascal castigated in his *Pensées*, has mutated into a new kind of intolerance.

This is what he wrote about freethinkers:

"Men despise religion; they hate it; and fear that it be true. To redress this bias, one should begin by showing that religion is not contrary to reason; that it is venerable, and worthy of respect, and then that one should see it as lovable, make the good people hope that it is true; and then show that it is true" (Brunschvicg, 187).

To freethinkers of the new observance who deny the reality of charismatas, signs and apparitions, this quotation should be transliterated in the following way:

"Men despise wonders of a religious nature; they hate them, and they fear that they may be true. To cure this apprehension, one should begin by showing that such wonders are not contrary to reason; that they are venerable, and worthy of respect, and that one should see them as desirable, and make the good people wish they were true, and then show that they do really take place."

My own reaction is that of Pascal: "How much do I hate doubters of miracles!" (*Pensées*, Brunschvicg 113). Such doubters withdraw the supporting columns of Catholic belief. It is to them that Heaven addresses the blistering philippic of La Salette:

"The priests, ministers of my Son, the priests, *by their lack of reverence and their impiety in the celebration of the holy mysteries,* through their love of money, their love of honors and pleasures, the priests *have become cesspools of impurity.*[92] Yes, the priests cry out for revenge, and vengeance is suspended above their heads. Woe to the priests and to the persons who are consecrated to God, who, through their infidelities and their loose life, crucify anew my Son! The sins of consecrated persons cry towards Heaven, and... since there is no one to implore for mercy and forgiveness for the people, there is no one left worthy to offer the stainless Victim to Eternal God in favor of the world." (My emphasis).

"If the salt have lost his savor, wherewith shall it be salted?" (Mt 5,13). If those whose ministry resides in the perpetuation of the wonder of the Eucharist shake of their allegiance to the reality of miracles, to whom can mere laymen turn? For every revelation is based on a miracle. There is nothing more authoritative than an utterance confirmed by a supernatural manifestation. Prophecies are believable when they are accompanied by a sign from Heaven. Who would believe in a talking bush? No one. But if that talking bush were on fire, and went on burning without ever falling into embers, cinders and ashes, one might assume with Moses that it was the mouthpiece for a heavenly message. Thus Moses believed in what the bush said, very much to his advantage and to that of his people.

Today, alas, bushes never talk, nor do they ever burn without consuming. But inanimate objects of a different nature speak a similar language. At Fatima, it was the falling sun that made of every one of the bystanders a living witness of God's message. What was that message? If mankind does

---

92 Mélanie seems to be alluding to these homosexuals who were ordained priest against what should have been the better judgment of the Seminary directors and who, as predators of the souls of the very young, brought the Catholic Church in America into disrepute and, through the resulting lawsuits, on the verge of financial ruin.

not repent and change its ways, a new war will break out worse than that of 1914.

Now, what is war? It is hell on earth, for it presupposes a devilish intent in every man bearing arms. While the devil wants to kill souls, the soldier wants to kill bodies. The main difference is that hell alone is forever. But the approximation is graphic enough. No student, however, can be taught against his will. And every nation-leader is inured by pride into learning from previous wars that there is no profit in starting a new one. If the seven plagues of Egypt left the Pharaoh unconvinced, how could World War I be an object lesson for a future Hitler or Stalin? And how about the seven plagues of the Apocalypse?

The first plague is already at work, for it is none other than the "first bowl of the wrath of God":

"So the first angel went and poured his bowl on the earth, and foul and evil sores came upon the men who bore the mark of the beast and worshipped its image" (Ap 16, 2).

Far from having learned that sin does not pay, men do not think Aids is the result of an immanent justice. Homosexuals are hardly aware that to practice what they deem as a birthright is an abeissance paid to the devil.

Shall modern man be made aware by ecological disasters that our earth has more ways than one to repay him in kind for the way in which he sullies its waters?

"The second angel poured out its bowl into the sea and it became like the blood of a dead man, and every living thing died that was in the sea" (Apoc 16, 3).

Never did British Petroleum assume it could have been chosen to give us a foretaste, offshore of Louisiana, of what is to happen to the oceans at large! Could not the methane on the sea-bottoms rise upwards to the surface, as a result of a warming-up of the oceans, to burst into flames as it comes to the surface? Thus would the prophecy of boiling seashores become reality.

Our present-day history is a reenactment of *Oedipus Rex* played backwards: the King has blinded himself even before reaping the consequences of his blindness. Mankind, with its loss of faith, has gouged out all possibility of supernatural vision.

"Supernature," nonetheless, is at work, spelling out its message in no uncertain terms. The world has already been judged, but the sentence has not yet been carried out. It has merely been intimated.

Those of us who are "not of this world" are aware of the unfolding drama. We have observed "the signs of the times." Pictures or statues of the Virgin have wept, either real tears, or tears of blood. Our Lady is concerned. And so is Christ, for his effigies too have shed tears of real blood.[93]

Thus, from January 4, 1974 to September 15, 1981 a wooden statue of the Virgin wept 101 times at Akita in Japan, in the convent of Sister Sasagawa. This phenomenon was Heaven's way of authenticating the messages this sister had received:

"My dear daughter... the Father Eternal is going to inflict a terrible punishment on all of mankind. It will be a greater punishment than the Deluge... Fire will fall from heaven and destroy a great part of humanity, sparing no one. The survivors will be so terrified as to envy the dead" (October 13, 1973).

Christians do not seem to be aware that they are running out of time. Neither does most of their clergy for that matter.

Thus at El Escorial, Christ could intimate:

"Woe unto you pastors who mutilate the Gospel, and

---

93 In both cases, the blood was the same as that on the Holy Shroud.

who do not teach men the truths that are to be found there... Many of you are civil servants, instead of being pastors of the sheep of Christ: you have an office in the world..."

As we have seen in previous chapters, the laws of probability are such that many of the people who are on earth today are on their way to hell. This is the situation which Christ addresses in his following warning to priests:

"Do not preach the Gospel according to your own personal choice, my children, preach the Gospel as it is... Preach the Gospel of Love and Mercy, but do not omit the God of Justice, the Judge of the Living and the Dead! How you conceal from men the word of hell, my children... My children, man can save himself out of love and out of fear." (Lk 1, 50; 2 Co 7,1; Ap 16, 7: 15,4).[94]

Self-interest is an irresistible argument. And in this respect, Mark Twain would have made a good Bible-thumping preacher, when he wrote:

"Of all the deterrents of temptation, the surest is cowardice."[95]

"Conscience doth make cowards of us all" (Shakespeare). It can also turn us into unwitting heroes. Soldiers have been known to face almost certain death on the battlefield rather than the firing-squad as deserters.

In her resourceful concern, Providence, as a measure of last resort, will appeal to man's instinctive self-interest. For his benefit, it will unveil the future and give him a foretaste of what the biblical "great tribulation" will be: a cataclysm such that there has never been a greater one before, and there will never be afterwards, barring the Last Judgment.

---

94 *L'Escorial: messages 1992-1998* (Association *Vierge des Douleurs du Pré-Neuf de l'Escorial*, F-64170 Artix, 1999: pp. 194-198).

95 As quoted by Joseph Sobran: "Finding evil," *The Wanderer*, May 24, 2001, p.6.

The Warning

When at the Cova da Iria, in 1917, the sun hurtled down towards a crowd of 50 000 unsuspecting onlookers, they cried out in terror, kneeled in supplication, begged for forgiveness. This was a mere dress-rehearsal for the "Warning" announced at Garabandal in 1956. This "Warning" indeed will have a cosmic dimension: from outer space a heavenly body will seemingly target the earth. In the ensuing panic, men should react as they did at Fatima. Panic, in its most acute form, quickens the conscience into an instant recall of the past, and in this case, with supernatural assistance, will awaken men into an immediate awareness of their sinfulness.

The Curé d'Ars once asked God to let him see his own soul, such as it was, with all its imperfections. He whose whole life had been one totally dedicated to God received nonetheless the answer that if his prayer were granted, the strain would be too great, and he would die.

Few men have the spiritual sensitivity of a Curé of Ars. Nonetheless, there will be some that will not survive the psychological stress of the self-knowledge brought about by the Warning.

There is thus an aggravation of terror between the crowd that panicked at Fatima, the whole human race confronted tomorrow with the unbearable realization of its wickedness by the Warning, and the subsequent Judgment of Nations executed upon the world at the first Parousia! In all three cases, the threat will have come from outside, while the perception of guilt comes from within. The Maker of the universe will have marshaled stars, comets and meteorites into instruments of immanent justice. It is written that he who lives by the sword perishes by the sword. Thus, he who lives in disorder, shall perish by the disordered violence of the elements. Such is the self-defeating nature of evil. This is what the seven plagues of the *Apocalypse* signify, each one in its own way, until the ultimate disaster. This lesson, to be learnt at the expense of two-thirds of mankind, will chasten the remaining third part into a deeper respect of natural law.[96] The shock will be such however that it is said that at first the survivors will "envy the dead."

From then on, for a millennium of peace, the harmony reigning in the platonic spheres will rule human behavior.[97] No longer will man be a wolf to man nor woman a harlot. Both will fulfill the purpose for which God quickened Adam out of primeval clay. The curse of Babel having been removed, "a civilization of love" will ensue, under the tutelage of angels. Mankind will glorify its Maker. "Paradise will have been regained," according to Milton's expression, minus the Adamic primeval innocence. There will be no return to the beginning, except as a term of reference, but the appropriate fulfillment of the Kingdom of God announced by Christ.

Thus, from the warning issued at La Salette through the timely recalls of Fatima, Garabandal, El Escorial, Medjugorje, Mandoria, Cua, San Sebastian, etc..., we Christians received precise instructions from the Virgin. The Mother of the Church fortifies our resolve. Her sons are not seduced into accepting the mark of the Beast, even if it means that

---

96 The culling by a disaster of cosmological size of some 5 billion people on earth may appear at first hand disproportionate to the crimes which brought about this result. Yet, on a regional basis, similar exterminations through natural disasters such as plagues have been almost current events in the course of history. In the 15th century, two thirds to three quarters of the Europeans died of the pest. And when their survivors reached the Americas, they were bearers of infections to which the natives were not immune. In Mexico alone 80 to 90 % of the local population died within one or two generations.

97 This is a metaphor.

they will be rejected from a society governed by the Antichrist.[98] All the while the Church will suffer from a division in its own ranks, unprecedented even in the days when there were three Popes.

What will the forthcoming trial of the Church be like?[99] For an answer to this question, see next chapter.

---

98 What will this mark of the Beast be like? Only those "who worshipped the Beast or its image" will be deemed worthy to receive this "mark on their foreheads or their hands" (Ap. 14, 9-10). This will not only be an honor, but it will be a practical necessity, since "no one can buy or sell unless he has the mark; that is, the name of the beast or the number of its name" (Ap 13, 16-18). That number is 666, which evokes for us the "www " of our electronic jargon, the "w" being the sixth letter of the Hebraic alphabet. Today, one hears rumors about the ominous implanting of an electronic microchip into the forearm of whoever wants to have access to banking privileges. The great advantage of this method is that it would permit governments to exercise perfect surveillance and control over world economy. What is far worse, however, is the possible working of nano-technology on the human psyche. Scientists have already succeeded in modifying the mood and dictating the behavior of rats with implants in their brain. While dictatorships of the past failed to exercise perfect mind-control with coercion, propaganda and brainwashing, those of the future may be more successful with this technology at their disposal.

99 As a rule of thumb surmise, we can foresee a falloff of two-thirds of the Catholics separating themselves from unity with the Pope: in other words, a major schism merely translating the already *de facto* lack of doctrinal orthodoxy of a majority of nominal Catholics.

**St. John devouring "the scroll" (Apoc. 10, 8-11),
Albrecht Dürer**

XV

SPONSA CHRISTI

Hope, which according to Father Bro "is the virtue of the future in the present," means placing one's trust in Providence. This attitude was noticeable among the Fathers of the last ecumenical council, in contrast with the less sanguine mood which followed, once the expected renewal had not taken place. The generation which came of age in 1968 would be for the Church "the lost generation" whose behavior Paul VI epitomized with the observation: "The smoke of Satan has entered into the Church." As if to counter this dramatic setback, in a broader perspective, he could evoke for the future a "civilization of love." In view of the long term, therefore, John Paul II could take up the challenge with his oft-quoted saying: "Do not fear." Benedict XVI, in turn, instilled a new feeling of purposefulness.

Whatever tomorrow may hold in store, it is reassuring to know that "the gates of Hell" will not prevail. We can only foresee, however, what is to come as a result of what has been.

If we consider mankind as a species without a transcendent destiny, we may well expect the worst at any given moment. Any random fragment of an exploding star, as it hurtles through space, could hit the earth. Christians, however, know "there is a providence in the fall of a sparrow." Are we "not worth more than a sparrow"? The most important single event in history is the one which we bracket with the letters *BC* and *AD*, the life of Christ being the measure of all things. At his death, from his open side, his Bride, the Church, was born. Tradition teaches us that her life shall be configured to that of her Spouse. Could then the persecutions the Church endured under Rome offer a parallel with the perils of His early childhood? Does not her "missionizing" of the pagan world recall His own preaching of the Kingdom of God? The Church has not yet, however, relived a trial similar in dramatic intensity to the Passion, Crucifixion and Death of Christ, even if there are countries such as Soviet Russia where the analogy applied on a local scale. As a personified whole therefore, the Church has not yet suffered, in intensity and universality, a fate comparable to that of her Lord and Master.[100] Are we to expect, that with the Antichrist replaying the part of Judas, she will be treacherously delivered unto her mortal enemies? Shall the institution embodying worldly power sit in judgment upon her as Pontius Pilate did with Christ? What will be her Road of the Cross? Shall she be mocked and scoffed at by her enemies as she lies stretched on the rack of persecutions? When will she rise again from what appears to be her demise?[101]

---

100 Israel has, however, in the course of the centuries, but more especially in the XXth, and anagogically, Israel stands for the Church.

101 Christ foretold to Maria Valtorta what the Passion of his Church would be:

."..she will know hours of darkness and of horrors similar to those of my Passion, multiplied in time, because it must be so.

It is necessary that the Church suffer as much as her Creator did... It is necessary that she suffer much longer, because, in her members, she is not perfect as her Creator was. And if I suffered

Many prophecies have foretold her future, as mentioned in various parts of this book. One recurrent theme has been the glory that will be hers once her enemies have been committed to hell. For such will be the fate of Satan and his evil spirits "for a thousand years." After which, these fiends shall be released for a short while, pending the return of Christ in His glory for the resurrection of the dead and the Last Judgment.

Thus, "one thousand years" before this ultimate quickening of the flesh, a "resurrection" of the Church will have taken place, as an event analogically related to that of Christ. Furthermore, did not Jesus, for forty days after Easter, comfort his followers with his visits before he rose to Heaven, from whence he sent them the Spirit of Consolation? Thus there shall be "a time" of the Holy Ghost as there has been " two times" of Christ. And the symbolism of numbers applies here in "thousands of years," those ascribed at first to the Father being foursome, as compared to the following twosome to Christ.[102] It is difficult to understand in which way this seemingly precise proportionality reflects what is proper to the Father, the Son

---

for hours, she will have to suffer during weeks and weeks of hours." (Maria Valtorta: *Les Cahiers de 1943*, Centro Editoriale Valtortiano, Isola del Liri, 2002, p. 181). If we compute this last figure, we come up with the following figures: 7x24=168=3.23, which coincides approximatively to the 42 months (3 years & ½) prophesied by Daniel and John. Furthermore, just as the Old Testament prefigures the New Testament, so should the holocaust of the People of the Word serve as a warning for the fate awaiting the People of Christ: 1962-1965 = three and a half years.

102 This is merely a loose application of mine concerning 12, 14 of the Apocalypse (and Daniel 7, 25): "a time, times and half-a-time," in reference to the interpretation of the mystic Luisa Piccarreta.

or the Holy Spirit in relation to the history of mankind. Let us remember, however, that in quantitative terms, it can be assumed that humanity, whatever disasters have now and then culled its numbers, increases and multiplies with the passage of time...

Is it not in these last "thousand years" that the prophecy of Christ to Nathanaël will come to fulfilment: "Amen, amen, I say to you: you shall see heaven opened, and the angels of God ascending and descending upon the Son of Man" (Jn 1, 51)? Bossuet comments on this as follows: "Why is it that Heaven is open? And what are these angels doing who ascend and descend with so light a flight, from earth to Heaven, from Heaven to earth? Earth is no longer in enmity with Heaven; Heaven is no longer contrary to earth: the path leading from one to the other is covered with blessed spirits, whose officious charity allows for a perfect communion between this place of pilgrimage and our heavenly fatherland."[103]

We stand presently, however, at that moment in time preceding the Passion of the Church, when crowds acclaim the Vicar of Christ wherever he goes. But it is a fleeting triumph, since the Church is yearly losing faithful by the hundreds of thousands to laxness in matters of morality and to relativism in questions of faith. When every third or fourth unborn child on earth is killed in the womb, and indifference to their plight is the current mood among Christians, we know that the forces of darkness are prevailing. Doubtless, the Passion of the Church is nigh...[104]

It shall be overcome in appearance, if not in reality. 'The

---

[103] As quoted in *"Magnificat"* (France) of October 2008, p. 383.

[104] Chapter written following a suggestion of Father Dietrich von Stockhausen, rector of the "Gebetstätte" of Heroldsbach.

happy few" survivors of persecution will find refuge in what the Apocalypse calls "the wilderness" in which the Woman clothed with the sun" seeks refuge for her child (Apoc. 12, 14-16).

What is her child, however, if not the Church?

The Angels restraining the four winds (Apoc. 7, 1-8), Albrecht Dürer

XVI

MARY'S ROLE

"In former times, the world was saved in Noah's ark. Today, my Mother is the Ark... He who rejects my Mother, rejects Me." (Our Lord on 30 Dec. 1989 at San Nicolas, Argentina).

I have already made the point that the Virgin of current apparitions, who understandably refers often to the Bible, especially in San Nicolas, nonetheless emphasizes that the *Apocalypse* applies specifically to our times. My numerous quotations from that book are thereby more than justified. But there are in the *Apocalypse* more allusions to the Virgin herself, and the role she plays in the economy of salvation today, than may meet the eye at first reading:

"Then I saw another angel ascend from the rising of the sun, with the seal of the living God, and he called with a loud voice to the four angels who had been given power to harm earth and sea, saying, "Do not harm the earth or the sea or the trees, till we have sealed the servants of our god upon their foreheads" (7, 2-3).

To the pilgrims of El Escorial in 1985-1988, this sounds familiar, for it evokes what Mary said: "...allow yourselves to be stamped with a seal," while Satan is applying his seal [on his own followers]...." Mary "has... received the mission of sealing the foreheads." For such is "the sign of election." It will "shine...on the day of Chastisement." 'You will see it then on one another.'"[105]

Thus, there are six more passages of the *Apocalypse*, where an angel, anagogically, stands vicariously for the Virgin Mary, fulfilling a task which can be said to be properly hers: 8, 3-5; 10, 1-11; 11, 3-12; 14, 6-7; 19, 17-21 and 20, 1-6.[106]

I will quote here merely the last reference:

"Then I saw an angel coming down from heaven, holding in his hand the key of the bottomless pit and a great chain. And he seized the dragon, that ancient serpent, who is the Devil and Satan, and bound him for a thousand years, and threw him into the pit, and shut it and sealed it over him, that he should deceive the nations no more, till the thousand years were ended. After that he must be loosed for a little while"(20, 1-6).

What is most significant here, in terms of Mariology, is that "the great chain" by which Satan will be bound can be said to be that of the rosary. This is the prayer which the Virgin has called upon us to say, time and again, in the various places where she is appearing. And the fervent way in which her request has been fulfilled is most edifying. In San Damiano, for instance, three times a day, three rosaries were recited, interspersed with hymns and invocations. Thus, without any sign of fatigue or boredom, the pilgrims spent daily a minimum of six hours in prayer. It is this unexpected capacity for endless prayer which is the gift of the Spirit to visitors at a place of apparitions.

This angel in the *Apocalypse* is a figure of the Virgin,

---

105 Gabriel: *Premier récit authentique des apparitions de l'Escorial* (François-Xavier de Guibert; Paris, 1996, pp. 333-334.

106 The anagogical interpretation of these six references, as for the one in the previous paragraph, was suggested to me by Mrs. Rita Malys.

according to the principle of anagogy - in other words if we search for the mystical meaning of the Holy Scripture. Mary, that very Woman designated in Genesis 3, 15, is shown here as the angel of mercy saving souls for the Coming of Christ. This is the very purpose she fulfills in her numberless apparitions today.

Is it not astonishing that she is never mentioned by name, not even once, in the *Apocalypse*, which is precisely the book she recommends us to read above all others, as the most appropriate for proper understanding of current events? She is present vicariously, however, through these angels who appear 7 times (see above) and play an important part.

Is it not already worthy of notice that she is only mentioned thrice in St. John's Gospel: at Cana for the miracle opening the way for her Son's mission, at Nazareth for the rejection of Jesus by his townsfolk, and at Golgotha when Jesus confides her to John as her adoptive son?

It is doubtless in fulfilment of his role, as Mary's second child, that John is so reticent to bring up the name of the Mother of Jesus in his writings. The other Evangelists are more explicit in their description of the part she plays. Doubtless because they had not been requested to leave her out. Mary, however, wished to remain in the shadow of her Son, as John the Baptist did after he had fulfilled his mission as prophet of the coming of Jesus: "He must increase, but I must decrease" (Jn 3, 30). (John the Baptist and Mary point to Jesus. The rest, as far as they are concerned, is silence. And the apostle John dutifully followed Mary's wish.)

Maria Valtorta, who can be said to have written a non-canonical, but surely an inspired work, understood that her prophetic task, on the eve of apocalyptic times, would be to highlight for our benefit Mary's co-redemptive mission.[107] She does this very effectively, and brings Mary out of the protective shadow she had chosen for herself out of humility, while she makes up for John's too literal observance of his Mother's wish.

For Mary stands now, with her hundreds of apparitions the world over, in the limelight of history.[108] She will fashion

---

107 Why "co-redemptive," when Christ alone is our Redeemer? - The answer to this question is beautifully expressed in the following quotation from St. Paul:

."..what is lacking of the sufferings of Christ I fill up in my flesh for his body, which is the Church..." (Col 1, 24).

When Paul deems that something is lacking in the redemptive effectiveness of Christ's Passion and Death, it is in the sense that it is only those who benefit from the message of the Gospel who can fully take advantage of it. Christ has dignified the function of the apostles to the point where they are called to share both his mission, not only in word, but in deed, and by participation to his calling through their own sufferings. A priest "saves soul" as does a victim-soul. Thus Mary through her "*fiat*" at the Annunciation collaborated so essentially to the Providential purpose of God that she should be called "*co-redemptrix*," just as she also deserves the title of "Mother of God."

108 Actually, "thousands of apparitions in recent times" would be more appropriate, according to Marco, the seer of Paratico (Close to Brescia, Italy. See *La Mamma del Amore*, I, June 6, 1997; p. 112): "Children, I appear in 7000 places all over the world: there will be even more; because the times have come in which Jesus wants to save mankind, He from whom mankind tries to distance itself. As for you, come to Him; do not say: 'Here the apparitions are authentic, and over there they aren't.' Listen to Mary's call, and when you listen with the heart, you will be saved." And on August 5, 1998: "Dear Children, the Holy Church does not manage to understand the return of Christ"(p. 143). On the 6th of January, Mary had been even more explicit: "Christ finds himself about to return in person, so as to separate good from evil, as the

history. She opens the eschatological chapter in her Son's post-resurrection biography, the one which he will write with earth-shattering wonders. She is the Prophet of the first parousia, that of the Judgment of Nations. Some of these nations, as we know, are condemned to disappear. Is Germany one of them? Probably at least in part, Hitler having tried to eliminate the chosen people in favor of the Germans...

France, astonishingly enough despite her role in fostering the spirit of revolution in the world, but as the crowning of her providential calling as "Oldest Daughter of the Church," will be saved, tells us the Mystic Marthe Robin (+ 1981), because God "will intervene through the Blessed Virgin. It is she who will save France and the world... [He] will intervene through the Blessed Virgin and the Holy Ghost: this shall be the new Pentecost, the second 'advent' of the Holy Ghost. A new era will start..."as confirmation of "the prophecy of Isaiah on the union of hearts and the unity of nations." [109]

Let us say with the *Apocalypse*: "Come, Lord Jesus," and rejoice at his Coming. For in the self-defeating consequence of the sin of pride, the Western World has chosen, through the new genocide of abortion, to cancel its own place in forthcoming history. We have to be saved from ourselves before we perish. "Come, Lord Jesus" before we drown in the sea of our sins.

And let us not entertain false hopes. The map of the world is to be redesigned, its magnetic field reversed, as probably its very axis, while its fauna and flora evolve in a

---

Holy Scripture says: "The one shall be taken, the other left behind."' (p. 99).

[109] Cf. Claude d'Elendil: *De Nostradamus à Alois Irlmaier* (Domus, p. 103).

non-Darwinian way. We shall hardly even recognize our-selves in the process, Mary having crushed the serpent's head beneath her foot, while men are spiritually reborn to a more obedient filiation in the Kingdom of God.

XVII

CONCLUSION[110]

"And Jerusalem will be trodden down by the Gentiles, until the times of the nations be fulfilled.

. . . .

Even so, when you see these things coming to pass, know that the Kingdom of God is at hand." (Lk 21; 24, 31)

At the beginning, the Dragon drew down in his fall "a third part" of the stars of heaven," which represent the angels whom the men are called upon to replace in God's following. Hence, the invitation to sanctity addressed to these *pauca minus ab angelis* who are asked to be "perfect, as also [the] Heavenly Father is perfect."[111] Now is the time to which the prophecy applies: "And it shall come to pass in the last days, says the Lord, that I will pour forth my Spirit upon all flesh" (Jl 2, 28).

The very apostasy of the "great number" will then be of advantage to the "small number," since the "faithful

---

110   As a form of self-plagiarism, this conclusion was lifted from another book of mine (*Is Mary appearing today?*: Goodbook media, Corpus Christi, 2018), since it is quite as topical in content in this one. If I am at fault, so was Rossini whose best tunes in *The Barber of Sevilla* were culled from his own previous operas.

111   "These *pauca minus ab angelis*" are "beings who are slightly inferior to angels": in other words, they are men.

servants" will receive, beyond those "talents" which they themselves have increased and multiplied, the super-numerary ones "taken away" from the "wicked and the slothful" who "had hidden them in the earth." If humor were conceivable in this context, one can readily imagine cohorts of angels busily engaged in digging out of the earth the talents, unprofitably hoarded up by the spiritually miserly, for redistribution to the deserving! (Mt 25, 14-30).

Nothing of what comes from God is wasted. The future profits from the past. Thus will the believers of tomorrow benefit, by providential adjudication, from the collective apostasy of the secularized nations of today. Even as we witness the fall-of of faith of the many, we are assured that this traditional belief, which they discarded as an old cloak, will have been hoarded by heavenly hosts to clothe in righteousness the yet unborn generations of tomorrow. This optimism is ours. It is also that of our XXth century Popes, even if they do not justify their expectations on the same grounds. They merely fulfill their prophetic mission without other qualification than that of their office.

Leo XIII, in somewhat conditional terms, opened the way:

"... the splendors of faith shall reappear, the swords will fall and the weapons will slip from the hands when all men accept the dominion of Christ and will submit to it with joy, and when "every tongue confesses that the Lord Jesus Christ is in the glory of God the Father" (*Annum sacrum*).

As for Pius XI, he declares that the institution of the feast of Christ, King of the universe, announces "the joys of the day when the human race of its own accord will submit to the very sweet sovereignty of Christ-the-King" (*Miserentissimus Redemptor*).

With Pius XII, the outline is more precise:

"How many hearts, o Lord, are expecting you! How many souls are pining away to hasten the day when you will live and reign alone in the hearts? Come, Lord Jesus, there are so many signs that your return is close" (Speech on the mystery of Easter, 1957).

And as another Hegel, he calls upon History, but on a

history favorable to the designs of the true Spirit:

"The birth, be it painful and prolonged, of a new life, of a humanity in constant progress in order and harmony, is the goal assigned by God to the history "post Christum natum," to which all the sons of God made free will have to contribute personally and actively." (Radio-message of Christmas, 1957).

John XXIII, about to convoke the Council, expresses "the definite resolution to return to certain ancient forms of doctrinal affirmation." Did he intend to revive the belief in the establishment of the Kingdom of God on earth, formerly entertained by the Apostles and celebrated by the early Church Fathers? In his eyes, the aim of Vatican II was to level "the road leading to the unity of mankind, necessary foundation for making of the terrestrial city the image of the heavenly city." And John XXIII evokes this theme once more in his speech for the closing of the first session, by prophesying that the "new long expected Pentecost" is none other than "a new leap forwards of the kingdom of God in the world."

Paul VI, more precisely, opposes to "the civilization of hatred" of our times this "civilization of love [that] will overcome the fever of relentless social conflicts and give to the world the so long awaited transfiguration of the ultimately Christian humanity."[112]

---

112 *Documents pontificaux de Paul VI (Discours de clôture de l'Année Sainte),* Ed. St Augustin, Saint-Maurice (Suisse), 1979, t. 14, p. 790. These social conflicts are unavoidable in an economy where the interests of capital and labor are conflictual, because they do not rest in the same hands. When will ownership and toil be shared and fulfilled by one and the same person? The utopias of state capitalism or unbridled liberalism have long enough ridden roughshod over the distinctive rights of the human person who can best find their accomplishment in what has only been timidly attempted up to now: a social structure responsabilizing the individual because he has his share in both property and work-load.

But it is John-Paul II who reveals, on the occasion of the Jubilee which marks the passage from the Second to the Third millennium, the very "fullness of meaning" and "the eschatological implication" of this "civilization of love," announced by Paul VI. Does not this latter expression describe to perfection the kingdom of God that we all hope for? And Paul Bouchard sees in it "the intuition that humanity is soon going to make its entry into the kingdom of God."[113]

These three Popes are quite explicit and to summarize what they have announced, we shall say with John XXIII: "We must prepare for the return of the Lord"; and with Paul VI: "The return of the Lord is imminent," while John-Paul II is even more emphatic: "We have entered the second Advent of the Church!"[114]

This theme which, from one pope to the next, is further developed bursts into heavenly strains when contemporary mystics take it up. And our Lord told to Josefa Menendez, "I want to reign." "I want to forgive souls and nations. I want to reign over nations and over the whole world. I want to spread my Peace until the extremities of the earth... I am Peace. I shall reign!"[115]

With Msgr. Ottavio Michelini (+ 1979), Jesus is even more explicit: ..."As it was said: "At the end, the merciful Heart of Jesus and the Immaculate Heart of Mary will triumph"... This is the way in which the advent of my reign on earth will take place... It will be, in other words, my intermediate coming... [which] will be invisible, in contrast to my first and my last coming, both of which visible... [It]

---

113 *Le Règne de Dieu sur la terre! Utopie ou réalité?* (Ed. Plurimédia/Parvis, Hauteville (Suisse), 1994, p. 145), which is a book to which I am indebted. *Cf.* also chapt. XIII of Paul Bouchard's *Les papes-prophètes du monde nouveau*, for the quotations of popes in this Conclusion.

114 According to the summary proposed by *Chrétiens magazine* (No. 238; mars 2011, p;18).

115 *Op. Cit.*, p. 148.

will constitute the Reign of Jesus in the souls."[116]

Even though the Coming will be invisible, the Reign will nonetheless be obvious, and Maria Valtorta paints it in glowing colors:

"O! My gifts! They will be felicitous for you! You will know neither famine, nor massacres, nor calamities. Your bodies, and even more souls, will feed on my manna; the earth will seem to rise again for a second creation, entirely new, in an atmosphere of peace and concord between the nations and of peace between heaven and earth, because I will pour on you plentifully of my Spirit, who penetrate you and give you the supernatural sight of God's decrees.

"It will be the Reign of the Spirit. The Reign of God, the one you ask for... in the 'Our Father'. Where would you want the Reign of God to come if not in your hearts? That is where my Reign on Earth must begin. A mighty reign, but nonetheless limited."[117]

---

116 *Id.* p. 157-158. And Msgr. Michelini reports the following words of Christ: "I confide to you once more, my son, the news of this hour of purification after which there will be a new Sky, a new Earth and a new Church. The decisive intervention of my Mother, Queen of Victories, will appear as evident to all, as will my own power and glory, true God and true Man. A new era will follow in the history of mankind." (p. 158)

"My intermediary coming...will be invisible," says our Lord here. But should we interpret literally, for this return of Christ, the expressions used by the various prophets? This would seem appropriate if, from one mystic to the next, uniformity had been the rule. This is hardly the case, however: other visionaries mention a huge cross in the sky, visible for the whole world, or, according to Luz Amparo, "Jesus will appear resplendent to all who shall be devoted to God and to his Very Holy Mother" (*L'Escorial, Messages 1992-1998*: Association *Vierge des Douleurs*, F-64170, 1999, p. 10).

117 *A l'aube d'une ère nouvelle, Prophéties de Jésus confiées à Maria Valtorta* (Centro Editoriale Valtortiano-Ed. du Parvis, Hauteville (Suisse), pp. 82-83, in the chapter 28, "Après la chute

Is it not meet and just that the mission of announcing the second coming of Christ has been especially entrusted to Mary? And that is what Saint Louis Grignion de Montfort expresses forcefully: "If therefore, as it is certain, the knowledge and the reign of Jesus-Christ will come to this world, it will only be as a necessary consequence of the knowledge and the reign of the most Holy Virgin Mary, who gave birth to him the first time and will make him known the second time." This sentence, which summarizes in three lines the thesis of this book, deserves to figure in the conclusion. Let us quote therefore the "little voices" to which our Mother or her Son entrusted their messages, with St. Michael's occasional intervention:

Thus spoke Mary to Gladys Quiroga de Motta, at Saint-Nicolas in Argentina, on Dec. 25, 1988: "Jesus came to this world out of Love and His Second Coming for His greater Glory will also take place because of Love."[118]

At Cochamba, in Bolivia, the Archangel reveals to Catalina in 1996 that "a new Kingdom is being readied for the Church and for the souls...The new terrestrial Jerusalem shall be as the commencement of the celestial Jerusalem."[119]

At Manduria, in Puglio (South Italy), in 1993, Debora conveys the following words on the part of Christ:

-- "I come to bring to earth the "New Pentecost."

-- "My project is to bring about the arrival of my Reign on earth as in heaven."

-- "She will soon descend in the midst of you, the New Jerusalem."[120]

And, on the part of the Virgin:

-- "I call upon everybody to proclaim that God is alive

de l'Antichrist: la Paix de Dieu").

118 René Laurentin: *Lire la Bible avec Marie, Messages de Notre Dame du Rosaire à San Nicolas* (F.-X. de Guibert, Paris, 1993, p. 378).

119 *La Grande Croisade de l'Amour, Messages de Jésus à Catalina* (Ed. du Parvis, Hauteville (Suisse), 1999, p. 295).

120 Christian Parmantier - André Castella: *Manduria* Ed. du Parvis, Hauteville (Suisse), 1999, pp. 123-126).

and that he is on the road of his return."

-- "Soon... the divine Light of the Very Holy Trinity will irradiate this earth and render her resplendent with purity. Then will my Son come back to edify the glorious Reign of his Father."[121]

What can be added after these quotes, if not the words of the Angel addressed to Mary concerning her Son and which she repeats when she appears here and there: "He shall reign"?

At Paray-le-Monial, in the 17th century, Christ speaking to Marguerite-Marie Alacoque, had been quite as specific: "I shall reign in spite of my enemies."

This is when all the requests of the prayer that Christ taught to us, the Our Father, shall have been satisfied:

1) God's name will be hallowed

2) since His Kingdom will have come

3) in which His will shall "be done on earth as it is in heaven"

4) while we receive "our daily bread": nourishment for body and food for soul

5) and live in a society in which "trespasses" against both God or man will be so slight as to be promptly forgotten by both God and man

6) since no one is led "into temptation"

---

121   *Id.*, pp. 145, 114-115.

If the above references are deemed untrustworthy because the visionaries mentioned have not (yet) been recognized, let me add that their prophecies are alike in content to those of so many saints that I could have readily supplied! Speaking in broad terms, these predictions are very much the same, whether they come from Garabandal, towards which the bishop of Santander was more than reticent, or from El Escurial, towards which the archbishop of Madrid was more than favorably disposed. Once again, circumstances can be detrimental or opportune, bishops however, as they come and go, tend as a rule, as times passes by, to be more impressed by the good fruits than distressed by the problematic character of what had seemed a novelty...

7) because our Tempter, "the Evil One," is serving a thousand-year sentence in hell.[122]

---

122 In the original text of the Our Father, the words "deliver us from 'evil'" can even more readily signify "deliver us from 'the Evil One'." This prayer is truly eschatological throughout.

ADDENDUM

The "Our Father" has never been as topical a prayer as today. What is, for instance, the full implication of its concluding words: "but deliver us from evil" if not "deliver us from the Evil One"?

For that last point is precisely what Providence has in mind.

Therefore let us rejoice, because the Prince of this World is about to lose his title, rule and domination.

He will not surrender, however, without a struggle that will shake the world to its foundations, while mankind quakes with fear...

This statement is to be taken literally, since, as prophesied by Vassula, earthquakes of 40 times their usual intensity will reduce our cities to rubble. A reversal of the axis of the world is foreseen. What is certain is that the fate announced for Babylon is paradigmatic for that of many a nation.

Do not take my word for it. What higher authority on this subject can there be than Sister Lucia of Fatima? This is how she reports what she learnt as she was kneeling in prayer before the Holy Sacrament on January 3, 1944:

"I felt a friendly hand, tender and maternal, touch my shoulder: I looked upwards and saw my beloved Heavenly Mother. ...

I felt suffused in a mysterious light which is God, and in Him I saw and I heard - from the point of a spear issues a flame reaching the axis of the earth - and while this axis quivers, mountains, towns and villages are swallowed up with their inhabitants. Sea, rivers and clouds, no longer bound to their proper domain, overflow, inundate and carry away in a vortex habitations and people in countless numbers: such is the purification of the world submerged in sin. Hate and ambition provoke destructive war!"

Is Lucia describing a cosmic disturbance, a nuclear conflict, or both?

She evokes then in less than two lines the thousand years mentioned in the Apocalypse (20, 4-6), before conjuring up in three words the ensuing Paradise:

"And then I perceived, midst the accelerated beatings of my blood and my spirit, the echo of a soft voice saying: 'In due time, one single faith, a single baptism, a single holy, catholic and apostolic Church. In eternity, Heaven!'"

St. John in his own text had been both more explicit and more mysterious:

"And I saw thrones, and they sat upon them, and judgment was given unto them: and I saw the souls of them that were beheaded for the witness of Jesus; and for the word of God, and which had not worshipped the beast, neither his image, neither had received his mark upon their foreheads, or in their hands; and they lived and reigned with Christ a thousand years.

But the rest of the dead lived not again until the thousand years were finished. This is the first resurrection.

Blessed and holy is he that hath part in the first resurrection: on such the second death hath no power, but they shall be priests of God and of Christ, and shall reign with him a thousand years" (Apoc 20, 4-6).

But as we shall see, this millennium will come to an end when Satan "shall be loosed out of his prison" (Id., 7).

What remains intriguing and awesomely wonderful is the role played by "they that were beheaded for the witness of Jesus," in other words, these martyrs who, having given testimony by their deaths, will resurrect and rule over a world chastened by disaster into a true worship of God... if only for a millennium.[123]

---

123 Should not the 21 Copts who in 2015 were beheaded in Libya for refusing to embrace Islam be considered a premise of

They will have died, the better to rule... after their martyrdom. What a paradox!

A heroic life leading to a premature death, after presumably a short delay of a few years - time enough for the brief reign of the Antichrist to implode -, then a coming back to life according to the pattern inaugurated by their Master, Jesus! Thus, it is as his ministers that they will fulfill their allotted mission.

They will bring Heaven on Earth, so to speak, as a reiteration of the time before the Fall, though not in perfect conformity with it, since men will not be born then as innocent as was the case with Adam and Eve. They will benefit, however, from the sacraments of a Church more responsive than it had ever been to its calling of Bride of Christ.

How could I ever do justice to the plentifulness of the promises of Christ to his Church?

No other communications of Heaven are as eloquent as those recorded in Vassula's book *True Life in God*:[124]

---

these martyrs? Their fate, recorded on television, was paradigmatic enough.

124 (On January 10, 1990). There seems to be no limit to the condescension of Heaven towards human frailty. Christ multiplies his visible interventions to convey his message in the most unconventional ways, as if to counter the later pseudo-miracles of the Antichrist, when men will watch, as if bemused by the show, signs as incredible as the conjuring tricks of magicians, yet, more effective than any man-made propaganda. Thus, it is with his own handwriting that we are told that Christ in this book is expressing himself. This is not a matter of Faith, but of observation, as with all supernatural manifestations in private revelations. We can take them, or leave them, at our own risk. But is there a risk in whatever edifies and brings us close to Gospel-truths? What we read in the Apocalypse is no less extraordinary. The revealed texts themselves dealing with our times take on an eschatological character, *id est* attuned to events which seem as earthshaking as Creation itself.

"... I am preparing you to live under the New Heavens and the New Earth because the time is drawing near now when Love is to return and live among you soon;

You shall hear Love's footsteps on the path of return, and it is for this reason all around the world My Voice is heard, and it is for the same reason your young ones see visions;

I have said that I will pour out My Spirit on all mankind and that your sons and daughters shall prophecy and that even to the least I will give my Blessings; yes, today my voice cries out in the wilderness, I am calling each one of you, yet some have failed to understand what my Spirit meant and have neither understood My Signs nor the visions of your young ones, they no longer count the fruits of Our Hearts but treat my chosen ones as impostors..."[125]

The most wondersome and explicit vision of things to come, however, is that of St. Irenaeus of Lyon (140-202), who championed an orthodox view of the future against that of the heretics of his days in his *Adversus Haereses:*[126]

"*John* has seen in advance the first resurrection, the resurrection of the Just, and the earthly inheritance proper to the Kingdom..." (p.24).

Then will the Just reign on earth, increasing in the following of the sight of the Lord; through Him, they will become accustomed to apprehend the glory of the Father and, in this Kingdom, they will have access to the holy angels and to the communion and the union to spiritual realities" (p. 58).

---

125 This lack of receptivity on the part of Christians focusing their attention on past visible interventions of the Spirit to the detriment of present ones mirrors that of the contemporaries of Christ who quoted the prophets the better to deafen the teachings of He whom the prophets had announced.

126 From Cyril Pasquier's book: *Aux portes de la gloire, Analyse théologique du millénarisme de saint Irénée de Lyon* (Academic Press Fribourg, Switzerland, 2008).

However, when...man will have been renewed, and he will be ready for incorruptibility to the point where he cannot age any more, 'it will be the new heaven and the new earth', in which the new man will live, conversing with God...(p. 70).

In the Kingdom, the just man living on earth will forget to die (p. 71).

...Then will the Just reign, after having been resurrected form the dead, and having been, as a result of this resurrection, showered with benefits by God (p. 97).

Those who receive the Spirit are as if in God's paradise (p. 110).

It is appropriate (...) that in the world in which they have been put to death because of their love for God, they should come back to life" (p. 117).

I think we should respect the mystery of the "how" of these marvelous proceedings through which God asks us to rejoice at the approach of the glory that will come to those who loved him more than their own lives.

Concerning the hierarchy between those who enjoy "the first resurrection" mentioned by St. John (Apoc 20, 6), and the Just of lesser standing, or even whoever might fit below them in this semi-paradise, St. Iraeneus leaves it up to us to imagine. If we try to draw definite conclusions from eschatological texts, we will remain in the dark. They are meant to edify rather than satisfy our curiosity; and the marvelous expression according to which death will seem more of an oversight than a necessity must be understood in the light of 1 Thes. 4, 16-17:

"...the dead in Christ will rise up first. Then we who live, who survive, shall be caught up together with them in clouds to meet the Lord in the air, and we shall always be with the Lord."

"And I saw an angel...having the key of the abyss and a great chain in his hand. And he laid hold on the dragon, the ancient serpent, who is the devil and Satan, and bound him for a thousand years. And he cast him into the abyss..." (Apoc 20, 2-3), Albrecht Dürer

ON THE END OF TIME

OR

THE LAST COMING OF CHRIST

Let us be reassured: the end of the world is not for tomorrow, but rather for after- tomorrow. For if we speak in biblical terms where a day is like a thousand years, then we are approximately that far removed from the dissolution of all things and from the resulting Heaven.[127]

As far as tomorrow is concerned, we know what to expect. Matthew has already told us so (ch. 24). The Disciples asked Christ:

"What sign will there be of the end of the age?"

Jesus was pretty explicit, while he seemed to want to reassure his listeners:

"You will hear of wars and reports of wars; see that you are not alarmed for these things must happen; but it will not

---

[127] As the Virgin announced in her apparitions at Hrushiv, Ukraine, in 1987 (April 2-August 15): "I have come to tell you that your sufferings will end soon. I shall protect you for the glory and the future of God's kingdom on earth, which will last for a thousand years. The Kingdom of Heaven and Earth is close at hand. It will come only through penance and the repentance of sins." When the Virgin corroborates what we have already learned from scriptural and traditional sources, what other arguments do we need to sustain our belief in a forthcoming 'civilization of love.'

yet be the end."

If the wars of today are still limited in scope, our time is ripe for their spreading in an uncontrollable way. And we have been told that this is precisely what will happen:

"Nation will rise against nation, and kingdom against kingdom; there will be famines and earthquakes from place to place."

For the world is like a pregnant woman for whom "all these things are the beginning of labor pains."

But the worst of what is to come takes on the form of a violent antagonism against true Christians, as a disguised metaphysical revolt against God and his Saints:

"They will hand you over to persecutions, and they will kill you. You will be hated by all nations because of my name. And then many will be led into sin: they will betray and hate one another. Many false prophets will arise and deceive many, and because of the increase in evildoing, the love of many will grow cold."

This does not mean, however, that the Just should give up hope:

"[For] he who perseveres to the end will be saved."

And he will be saved, either because he died the death of a witness of Christ, or because he was protected from harm for the benefit of "the Kingdom of God on earth" in which he will enter as a result of the Second and Intermediate Return of Christ.

This Return will bring about the Kingdom for which Christians have been praying for centuries in their "Our Father":

"May thy kingdom come."

For this accomplishment of God's will, however, "on earth as it is in heaven," one condition is necessary: the conversion of heretics and heathens. And this will happen: "[once] this gospel of the kingdom [has been] preached throughout the world as a witness to all nations."

This prophecy, seen from the present perspective, can be understood in two ways:

1) either as a tentative process which has already happened in the person of John-Paul II who traveled

the world over to bring "the good news" to a hundred countries;

2) or as a completed process which will take place on the morn of the forthcoming "millennium," after Satan has been locked up in hell "for a thousand years."

In our chapters on the Intermediate Return of Christ, we have already described how humanity will collectively observe the moral law as never before. This holiness of the many has been announced in the Old and the New Testaments and this teaching has been relayed by the Early Fathers of the Church and since then by mystics and saints. In our days, the Mother of Christ, in countless apparitions, has promised the Triumph of the Eucharist and of her Immaculate Heart, while Satan is confined to hell.

Such will indeed be the status of the Church of Philadelphia, according to the *Apocalypse*:

"Because thou hast kept the word of my patience, I will also keep thee from the hour of temptation, which shall come upon all the world, to try them that dwell upon the earth" (3, 10).

Now the Church of Philadelphia should be of great interest to us, because we are part of it. It is our Church, as distinct from the Church of Sardis which preceded it, or the Church of Laodicea which will follow. For there are seven Churches, according to St. John, which represent the 7 phases through which our one and only Mother Church goes through until she is replaced by the Heavenly Jerusalem after the Last Judgment.

Loosely translated the "Church of Philadelphia" means "the city of love." Shouldn't we rejoice and celebrate at the thought that we are called to live in it? For the time being, however, we are faced with "the hour of temptation which shall come upon all the world," when the Church, confronted by the most hostile environment of its history, will survive as if through fire.

Phoenix-like, however, its embers will ignite upon our planet the greatest conflagration of love of its history.

But since "the figure of this world" will pass inevitably, this millennium of the "civilization of love" shall come to an end as a result of the most insidious of all temptations: that of indifference that will blight the faith of its follower, the ultimate and last Church on earth, that of Laodicea:

"I know thy works, that thou art neither hot nor cold: I would that thou wert hot or cold," sayeth the Lord.

"So then, because thou art lukewarm, and neither cold nor hot, I will spue you out of my mouth"(Apoc 3, 15-16).

By then, Satan will have been "loosed" from hell for "a little season" (Apoc 20, 3).

But since this will be his own last and ultimate release from the confines of his subterranean kingdom, he will make the most of this "holiday from hell." Galvanized by the urgency of the occasion, he will inspire in men, as said before, a spirit of indifference to transcendent values, so as to neutralize spiritual defense mechanisms. In other words, he will follow exactly the same pattern of subversion to which he owed, in our own times, his first momentary and almost total triumph among the greatest part of the world's population. It is as if the prophecies which apply to our immediate future, with a few exceptions, are also fully relevant for the last generation of humans. That is why the Evangelists, and since then countless interpreters of the Holy Scriptures, have had such a hard time differentiating the predictions applying to the eve of the First Return of Christ from those which deal with the dawn of his final Return. What is specific to the latter, for instance, is the identity of the Antichrist. His name could have been most appropriately "Gog" as in derision for "God," if this term had not been conferred to one of the rebellious nations who march under his command. Personally, he will be none other than the Devil and come presumably disguised as a human being. Since the evil one's powers and capacities, stupendous as they are, are nonetheless finite - bounded as they are by nature and divine decree -, he will have to rely on his old bag of dirty tricks and repeat, with a thrice exponential effectiveness, the performance which had already been rehearsed for him in our century by his forerunner, Antichrist number one. For this first attempt at total subversion will be a kind of foreplay of his own final fling.

Since we have not yet witnessed the first vicarious triumph of Satan, at which we can only surmise on the basis of the proximate triumph of his first human counterpart, we cannot describe his own short-term ultimate and final triumph, except as a magnified projection of what we are soon to experience. We have to rely on announcements made in the traditional language of eschatology, most typically in those of Daniel, whose vocabulary is more figurative than analytical. Evil is repetitive in its essence, even when, with the fundamental ambivalence of temptation, it takes on a hue of novelty. *Nihil novum sub sole.* Satan's plan is to infect mankind with the virus of despair, after having deluded it with the promise of instant gratification. Thus humanity is about to go through the claustrophobic experience inflicted to souls in hell, appropriately adapted to conditions on earth.

"And the kings of the earth, and the great men, and the rich men, and the chief captains, and the mighty men, and every bondsman, and every free man, hid themselves in the dens and in the rocks of the mountains:

And said to the mountains and rocks, Fall on us, and hide us from the face of him that sitteth on the throne; and from the wrath of the Lamb:

For the great day of his wrath is come, and who shall be able to stand" (Apoc. 6, 15-16).

Though this text applies literally to the end of the world, when "the heaven departs as a scroll when it is rolled together," and time is about to be canceled, it is also prophetically reminiscent of the warning of Christ to the women of Jerusalem:

"For, behold, the days are coming, in which... [your children] shall begin to say to the mountains, 'Fall on us', and to the hills, 'Cover us'" (Luke, 23, 29-30).

These verses from the Apocalypse and Luke should soon become topical for us too.

To reject Christ is to seal one's own fate and compromise the future of further generations, as in the case of the Jews two thousand years ago or in that of the nominal Christians of today. For if the Jews were not aware that by rejecting Christ they were rejecting God, the Christian nations, when they refuse to acknowledge their Christian heritage, do not suspect they are also refusing God's providential tutelage. Or even worse, they do not care, for they are not aware that Christ's warning was addressed to them: "Without me, you can do nothing" (Jn 15, 5). God will not save us against our will from the consequences of our own vagaries. When we have, with our inordinate plunder of natural resources, compromised the future of that very life that sustains us on earth, can we expect to escape miraculously from the resultant disasters? Our planet will not provide a safe haven for those who have contaminated its very atmosphere or polluted its waters.[128] The hair-raising scenario of worldwide accelerated increase of temperature is well-known. We fail, however, to take concurrently into account the forthcoming cataclysms of cosmic origin announced in the prophecies. Our scientists have described both types of catastrophes, between which, in spite of their disregard of biblical warnings, they can tell us what is plausible and what is merely possible. They do not realize that, besides what is plausible because of ecological irresponsibility, what is hypothetical can occur also because of moral deviancy. Sodom and Gomorrah are a case in point. Mankind, in the meantime, is toying blindly with means of self-destruction. We have weapons today that are as dangerous as a loaded

---

128 Women curb their fertility with pills whose synthetic non-biodegradable elements, once eliminated, affect the fishes in the rivers, the birds in the estuaries, and even the polar bears! Similarly, in the last forty years, the sperm-count of men has been reduced noticeably while the number of unwillingly childless couples has doubled. In the sterile atmosphere of pharmaceutical firms, male employees who worked on the manufacture of these pills had to be removed because their breasts grew while they started experiencing same-sex attraction. Thus, the present exponential increase of homosexuality should be ascribed, initially, to homeopathic traces of estrogen in nature. No one mentions, however, what all should know, and no measures are taken to prevent what threatens the future of mankind.

pistol in the hand of a madman.[129] We do not realize that nations are as likely as individuals to lose their mind: communities can become clinically sick, purely as a result of aberrant ideologies. They are then led by leaders who, as incarnations of the *Zeitgeist*, minor Antichrists such as Hitler or Stalin, institute reigns of terror and reap destruction for both opponents and followers.[130] Men have to be saved from themselves, and that is what meteorites hurtling towards earth, or some huge celestial body brushing past our planet, masterminded by a providential purpose, can achieve by the very simple process of destroying both modern technology, and the life-standard it provides.

Whatever the future has in store, let us rejoice nonetheless "for our liberation is at hand." Once wars, famines, persecutions and heavenly retribution have reduced our cities to rubbles, humanity will have cause to breathe a

---

129 No less than twice in the last fifty years, the world was saved from a nuclear war, by the refusal of a subordinate to follow the order given by his commander: once in a Russian submarine during the Cuba crisis by the officer in charge of firing an atomic torpedo, and a second time in Siberia when the captain told to press the fatal button of global retaliation declined to believe that the signals sent by a satellite, which recorded five flashes of oncoming missiles from the United States, were genuine. As a result of disobeying official orders, said captain was demoted. Not to mention the case, when rats gnawing at a cable almost provoked the accidental firing of an intercontinental missile. Humanity is toying with total disaster as an almost routine occurrence. We in the West do not seem to be aware that this teetering on the edge of atomic annihilation has in two further occurrences resulted in a breather of peace: first in Siberia when at a testing of its last *nec plus ultra* missile, Russia lost in an accidental explosion a whole generation of generals and experts; and the second time in Murmansk when the whole stockpiled ballistic missiles similarly blew up.

130 It is hard to believe that, as Antichrists, these two monsters were pale adumbrations of the forthcoming one.

sigh of relief, not only because the worst is over, but at the gratifying discovery that Satan's reign is over too.

"I saw Satan fall from the sky like a lightning," said Christ announcing the coming of the Kingdom of God (Lc 10, 18)

He announced it, and it came as a result of Christ's sacrifice, and it was lived, as announced, in the lives of saints: "The Kingdom of God is within you." And yet, this was an individual thing, in spite of the Church, the Spouse of Christ. For though the power of Satan has been reduced, he retains his hold over the world of which he is still the Prince. [131]

Another turning point in history, therefore, two thousand years after Christ, will be Satan's arrest and confinement. This time, however, this overthrow of his will follow closely on the heels of what should have been his crowning success, the apparent demise of the Church under the tyrannical reign of his *alter ego*, Antichrist number one.

Just as the Holocaust, with its six million victims, heralded the return of Israel to the Promised Land, the bloody Passion of the Bride of Christ will bring to a close an era of evil with the forthcoming millennium of peace. Figuratively, Israel and the Church are one and the same, but in consecutive order.

"And I saw an angel come down from heaven, having the key of the bottomless pit and a great chain in his hand.

And he laid hold on the dragon, that old serpent, which is the Devil and Satan, and bound him a thousand years.

And cast him into the bottomless pit, and shut him up, and set a seal upon him, that he should deceive the nations no more, till the thousand years should be fulfilled..." (Apoc 20, 1-3).

I suspect few of us adequately realize how much we will owe to Archangel Michael's intervention! For the first time since Adam's Fall, the Serpent shall be banned from that

---

131 That is why, in spite of the widespread growth of the Church in the Western World, so much of the antique barbarity of man remained, even in the very Christian Middle Ages.

very earth to which he had been relegated as punishment:

"And the Lord God said unto the serpent. Because thou hast done this, thou art cursed above all cattle, and above every beast of the field; upon thy belly shalt thou go, and dust shalt thou eat all the days of thy life" (Gen 3, 14).

Every triumph of Satan is self-defeating, and he has paid a bitter price for a strategic victory in Eden over one weaker than himself. What does it mean for a pure spirit to move reptilian-like "upon his belly" and eat dust "all the days" of his life? This esthetic disgrace for a twice-fallen angel signifies some degrading submission to a contingency he has to share with corporeal entities. His angel's wings were clipped and he entered a new and ominous relationship with time and space. Imagine his anger, furthermore, at hearing what follows:

"And I will put enmity between thee and the woman; and between thy seed and her seed, it shall bruise thy head, and thou shalt bruise his heel" (Id., 4).

The enmity was already there, for Satan had initiated it, but that the very biped he had duped, should bruise his head was hard to bear. It meant he would be wounded in his pride, at the very heart of his purpose.

If he understood the first part of the sentence meted out to him by God in verse 3, since its execution was instantaneous I doubt he really could fathom at this stage what would be the full implication of the second part in verse 4: i.e. the part the Virgin would play in it, such as it is expressed in the prophetic reading of the following verse: "She shall tread on your head and thou shalt bruise her heel."

He would discover what this meant, as time went by, step by step. We need not spell out what took place, since for him and us it is now past history. What awaits us both, however, is so drastic a change in our relation to one another that it deserves explanation. When the thousand-year lockup prevents the dragon from roaming around *sicut leo quaerens quem devoret*, how great will be our relief!

It is said the young Masai only reaches full manhood when he has killed a lion with a spear. Similarly, humanity will enjoy the full adulthood of the children of God, when it is no longer stalked at every step by soul-eating invisible fiends.

Today, however, when they are still preyed upon by devils, lapsed Christians have imagined, as solace for their bruised egos, the nonexistence of these enemies of theirs which trip them into sin. Such disbelief has aberrant psychological consequences, since they cannot repeat what Eve said : "I was deluded by the devil." We cannot disclaim our own responsibility when we no longer have any one to share it with. And we have to face the despairing conclusion that, left to ourselves, we are hopelessly bad, unless we choose, with even greater duplicity, to deny that we have sinned in the first place. Sin is no longer sinful in the eyes of those men who, after disbelieving in the devil, negate God as the Supreme Creator towards which they are beholden and accountable.

However, even in this situation, we are sometimes shaken out of our blind complacency by some inadvertent faux-pas of the evil one. For instance, when his pride gets the better of him. Father Amorth, the exorcist of Rome, tells the story of this priest who asked to attend an exorcism in spite of the fact he was skeptical of the whole proceedings. As soon as he showed up, the devil laughed at him: "Aha, you do not believe in me, but you believe in girls." The red-faced skeptic beat a hasty retreat. Here the devil, hurt in his pride, surrendered his anonymity for the benefit of a "bon mot," even if it meant jeopardizing a priceless asset to his own cause.

In the same way, if the general opinion is that evil spirits are a myth, there is also, almost contrariwise, a widespread belief in spiritualism, black magic, superstition, divination, spells, etc... The devil that has been banned is called upon, as it were anonymously, to play a part, to render a service, either to prove that he is better than his reputation, or as fulfilling his role of messenger of hate.

The most overlooked office of Satan, however, is the one he exercises as "god of this era" (2 Cor 4; 4) or "Prince of this World," and of which he boasts to Christ when he tempts him in the desert:

"He...shewed unto him all the kingdoms of the world in a moment of time, and [he] said unto him. All this power will I give thee, and the glory of them: for that is delivered unto me; and to whomsoever I will give it" (Lk 4, 5-7).

Thus, it is both in the intimate realm of the individual conscience, and on the level of society and nations, that Satan holds sway, when we give him leave to do so. That this is the case today in an unprecedented way is obvious to anyone who turns on his television set. While the private viewer submits to a subtle and pernicious mind-control, the citizen is called to conform in public to standards set by what is "politically correct." Correspondingly, the decline of faith and worship of man as collective model imperils that very purpose of Creation and Incarnation which is the intimacy of God and man. At this lowest moral ebb in the history of this planet of ours, our Father who is in heaven will inflict upon our "Babylon" the greatest chastisement of all time. This is what Scripture calls that "great tribulation" (Mt 24, 21), which for the prophets and mystics of recent centuries are "the three days of darkness." Such is the catastrophe during which the Antichrist, Satan and his human minions will all be confined to Hell. Once Satan is under lock and key "for a thousand years" (Apoc 20, 2), however, the survivors on earth of these "three days of darkness" will be overcome by the realization that something unprecedented has happened, and not only because of the dramatic events they have gone through. Imagine the amazement of men when they discover that, in the intimacy of their own conscience, or in their relation to one another, sin and strife have lost their hold, as if the burden of daily or occasional temptations had been removed. It is not, however, that men will have suddenly been reborn without the concupiscence originating from Adam's Fall, but that they will no longer be tripped into sin by the constant solicitations originating from those invisible escorts of theirs, the devils...

Eve showed how foolish she could be when she believed the Serpent. Though we are certainly more foolish than she or even more conceited than Adam in their state of innocence, we nonetheless lack, as mere humans, the capacity to choose evil for its own sake, since this ultimate subversion of motivation can only be found in hell. Once the doors of this infernal abode have been sealed for a thousand years, the workings of grace will no longer be hindered as if *ab extra*. The efficacy of the sacraments will be multiplied. No desert will have been conjured into a sea of flowers, after a long awaited rain, with a more multicolored splendor than men's souls. And saints will there be in such abundance that the registers of canonization can no longer keep track of them. Cathedrals will dot the landscape way beyond the wildest dreams of devout medieval Church-builders.

There is a place in Normandy, Tilly-sur-Seulles, where the Madonna in 1896-99, announced that a huge Basilica should be built, which she showed not only to the nuns and the children of the local school, but described in greater detail to the visionary Marie Martel.[132] If, in spite of miracles and wonders, nothing lasting came of these apparitions, because of the opposition of the bishop, too many of the prophetic announcements made by Marie Martel have since been corroborated. In this respect also, what should have been done in the past shall be done in the future. And Tilly-sur-Seulles will be better known than Lourdes.

For at last the Church, with all its hierarchy, will render full homage to the more than hundreds of Marian apparitions which have taken place in the last century and up to now. Mary precedes Jesus as the dawn announces the day. We are expecting the return of Christ: "Come Lord Jesus."

It will be His reign and most especially that of the Holy Ghost, whose gifts will be granted to men of good will with an unprecedented generosity. In this later respect, God cannot be trumped, and He has stored century-long gratuities for us in the expectation of this hour. These are the generations in whose "lap" a "good measure" will be poured, "pressed down, shaken together and running over" (Lk 6,

---

132 The same promise was made at San Damiano in Italy where the Virgin appeared in 1961-1981.

38).

Since this earth, however, is no permanent abode for mankind, our statute of tenancy will run out one day. Men will be made aware of the imminence of this foreclosure of occupancy by the sudden realization that they are no longer at peace either with one another, or with themselves. This invisible intrusion of a spirit of strife will accompany the return of Satan, "loosed out of" the prison in which he has served out his thousand-year sentence.

"And [Satan] shall go out to deceive the nations which are in the four quarters of the earth, Gog and Magog, to gather them together to battle: the number of whom is as the sand of the sea.

And they went up on the breadth of the earth, and compassed the camp of the saints about, and the beloved city: and fire came down from God out of heaven, and devoured them" (Apoc 20, 7-9).

Thus we are told very little of what will happen at this short terminal point of history. When the Apocalypse enters into a lengthy enumeration of plagues, we tend to interpret them as applying to "the end-times," these times we are entering as of today, as if they coincided with "the time of the end." We are more concerned about the disasters which concern us personally. According to Maria Valtorta, however, this upheaval of nature against man, and of men against each other, resulting from Satan's increasing intervention in the affairs of this world, will be very much the same in both cases. The difference is that it shall reach a manifold intensity towards the end of time.[133] Thus we can read the

___

133 Jean-Marie Mathiot concurs: "The painful events that precede the spiritual Reign of Christ - which will be followed by the coming of Antichrist [number two] - are the general and analogous repetition of the events that will precede the end of time and the Parousia" (*Vues du Ciel, Prophéties pour aujourd'hui et pour demain*: Parvis, Hauteville (Suisse), 2012, pp. 20-21). First comes the blue-print, then the original. As it was for the Judgment of Nations, so shall it be for the Final Judgment: similar signs announcing them, but worse in the second case.

following description as applying both to the immediate and to the more distant future. God speaks here in His own name, since what He announces results from His own direct intervention:

"I will work wonders in the heavens above and signs in the earth below, blood, fire and a cloud of smoke. The sun shall be turned into darkness, and the moon to blood, before the coming of the great and splendid day of the Lord, and it shall be that everyone shall be saved who calls on the name of the Lord" (Acts 2, 19-21).

Let us meditate upon the words of mercy by which God concludes his message, since their salvifying efficacy depends on our belief in God's love. The ability to interpret the worst tribulations as redemptive trials is only given to those who, such as Dismas the good thief on the cross, pray with utter conviction:

"Lord, remember me when you enter into your Kingdom."

For it is indeed the total abolition of earthly hope that allows for a genuine trust in what is not of this world.

The bad thief lapses into despair, however, for he blasphemes. Blasphemy denies that God saves whoever is willing to be saved. Whatever the circumstance, damnation is always self-inflicted. Justice is the retribution we owe to ourselves.

The minor prophet Joel, is a graduate in the science of eschatology. And this is what he has to say:

"The Day of the Lord is coming: a day of darkness and of gloom like dawn spreading over the mountains, a people numerous and mighty!.. Their like has not been seen from of old, nor will it be after them... before them fire devours" (2, 1-3).

He is alluding to the armies spurred on by Satan, Gog and Magog, recruited among candidates for hell, as if anyone but a madman could choose safety in numbers. Might is the argument which appeals most to those who are so self-centered that they want to be on the winning side. They are merely repeating the mistake of Judas.

If a prophet like Joel, who lived in the 4th century

before Christ, can show concern for events relating to the end of the world, the interest which Paul shows for the events preceding the Intermediate return of Christ may seem more relevant to us:

"With regard to the coming of the Lord Jesus Christ... (that day will not come) unless the apostasy comes first and the lawless one is revealed, the one doomed to perdition, who opposes and exalts himself above every so-called god and object of worship, so as to seat himself in the temple of God, claiming that he is a god... whom the Lord [Jesus] will kill with the breath of his mouth and render powerless by the manifestation of his coming" (2 Thes 2, 1-8).

That this text applies to Antichrist number one is made clear by the fact he is killed, which proves that he is flesh-bound. As such he merely claims that he is "a god." The pretense of being God Himself is one which Satan does not delegate. He tried his hand at it at the beginning. At which point he was defeated by Michael's cry: "Who is like God?" He has been bidding his time since then, waiting for the favorable occasion to renew his attempt at scaling the skies. He knows that it is all pretense and sham. But mankind is gullible. And on the narrow stage to which he is confined, Satan will put on a deceitful show which his display of power will make believable. The last Antichrist will be he, presenting himself as no one other than the real Man-God. I would have to be as clever as he is himself to be able to explain by which device he will flesh out a Man-Devil convincingly enough to reach such a pinnacle of deception. This is the "desolating abomination... in the holy place... spoken of through Daniel." Jerusalem apparently is to be showcase of this supreme expression of unbridled pride.

When television achieves the three-dimensional quality to which it is striving, the virtual world of entertainment will offer but a pale idea of what we are to expect in terms of collective illusion.

In the eyes of men, will Satan achieve the grandeur of the *persona* Milton conferred to him in his epic poem? All the resources of art and science, magnified into a display worthy of such an enterprise, cannot disguise that Satan simulating a Messianic destiny is little more than a parody. That there will be men gullible enough to pay the necessary entrance-fee of sin to play a part in this supreme drama of self-deception is a mystery... the very mystery of evil.

It is not as if we had not initiated the process that will lead to our own collective undoing. Maria Valtorta tells us how this will happen:

"When impiety and injustice sway the inclinations of 99% of humanity, when ungodliness, intellectual presumption and material unlawfulness overrun all social classes, and when abomination has even infiltrated the house of God - this abomination of the desolation of which the prophet speaks..., God will no longer correct you with paternal chastisements which, truly speaking, only save a few. Since the greatest number are already Satan's retainers, HE WILL DELIVER YOU UNTO YOURSELVES. He will withdraw. He shall no longer intervene. Until the moment when, with a flash of His will, He shall order His angels to break the seven seals, sound the four trumpets, free the eagle of the three disasters, after which, horror! the fifth trumpet shall sound, and the Judas of the last times will open the infernal abyss to release what man hath desired more than God."[134]

How mere humans such as "the Judas of the last times" can yield enough power to release from hell "what man hath desired more than God" is a mystery. Is it possible that treachery reaches such proportions that God's immanent justice will allow mankind to reap the fruit of prevarication through Satan's return? We have seen in our times what happens when godless tyrants are elected to power. We shall see then what happens when majority choice votes for the Evil One in person. "When will that happen?" asks Maria Valtorta.

"The moment will not be revealed to us. It is registered in the heart of the prophets of today. 'But what the seven

---

134 Maria Valtorta as quoted by Gabriele M. Roschini in *La Vierge Marie dans l'Oeuvre de Maria Valtorta* (Centro editoriale valtortiano, Isola-del-Liri, 2010, p. 362-363).

thunders have told.... is sealed and will not be revealed" (see Ap 10, 4). And then, *as a star of peace above the horror and the terror of the tempestuous waves "* - (since only the passengers in the bark of Peter will escape shipwreck) - *the dawn of the Star of the Sea* will rise... This will be the last apparition of the Morning Star. In his second and last return, the Lamb of God... will not have for precursor" John the Baptist. *He will have our Angel for precursor, she who was a Seraphim in the flesh, she in whom we have established our residence...*, the beloved Ark of pure gold that contains us as she is contained by us and who shall cross heavens in her flight, radiating her love to prepare the royal... way, and to engender and give birth in an ultimate maternity all those ... who will want to be brought forth in the Lord..."

Such is the metaphoric language in which Valtorta describes how, she who is our succor "at the hour of our death," is also the one through whose ministration we are born unto the Lord at this hour of the world's greatest and ultimate peril.

We all know the part played by Mary to prepare us for the second coming of Christ: her numerous apparitions at Garabandal, l'Escorial, Manduria, Medjugorje, Schio, San Nicolas, Cua, Amsterdam, Naju, Akita, Brindisi, etc... the world over. She did not neglect a fleck of earth. She spoke to all of us, even if the response of Christians in general and their leaders in particular has been muted by conformity, prejudice, routine or plain indifference. She even addressed herself silently to the Copts and the Moslems in those hundreds of apparitions in Zeitoun (Cairo) and elsewhere in Egypt, where she was witnessed by hundreds of thousands and visible on television.[135]

---

[135] There is safety in numbers, and such was also the case when at Hrushiv, Ukraine, in 1987 she appeared to a total of as much as a half-million within two weeks. "Neither the Soviet militia could begin to manage the crowds. The Virgin Mary was even seen by the KGB agents!" (http://www.divinemysteries.info/our-lady-of-the-ukraine-hrushiv-ukraine-1914-and-1987).

Now, St. Grignion the Montfort, as the prophet of Mary for today, is no less eloquent and convincing when we read him with the end of the world in mind:

"...the greatest Saints... will be most assiduous in their prayers to the Very Holy Virgin... I have said that this would happen especially at the end of the world... It is through Mary that the salvation of the world began and it is through Mary that it must be consummated... God wants therefore to reveal... Mary, the masterpiece of his hands, in these last times..."[136]

As we see, though I have entitled this ultimate chapter the "The Last Return of Christ," I will have mostly been describing events relating to His Intermediate Return. The reason for this is that the Intermediate Return is for us an object lesson for the Final Return. The more we know about the one, the better we will understand the latter. The pattern of disasters preceding the first Parousia, terrible as it is already, is but a mild foretaste of those preceding the second Parousia.

There are few events that can be sequentially situated with as much precision in the Apocalypse as the Last Return of Christ, since it stands for the End of History. St. John mentions it in chapter 20, and then, within three chapters, describes what will take place. That is truly very little space in which to do justice to the limitless "Now" of happiness which is to wipe all tears from men's eyes.

At this point, comments are unnecessary. St. John, from his retreat in Patmos, sees the glorious future of the redeemed and resurrected part of humanity unfolding under his very eyes, while death, suffering and purgatory are mere memories, and the impermanence of appearance no longer disguises the supernatural unity of truth, love and beauty:

"And I saw a new heaven and a new earth..." (Apoc 21,

---

136 *Traité de la Vraie Dévotion* in *Oeuvres complètes de Saint-Louis Grignion de Montfort* (Paris, Ed. du Seuil, 1966, pp. 512-515).

1).[137]

No one here can improve on the original text in sublimity. This descent from Heaven of the Bride of Christ as a city of radiance and precious stones, follows the Last Judgment which we can best summarize as a Judgment of Love.[138]

For all men, will be judged according to the conformity of their lives with the ten commandments, but most especially with the first two:

"Thou shalt love the Lord thy God with all thy heart, with all thy strength and above all things."

For those men, whose love for a God they did not know of, was merely implicit, the Second Commandment serves as a substitute to the First:

'Thou shalt love thy neighbor like thyself."

The Saints, however, as a special class, will be greeted and praised by the Lord for the conformity of their lives to what I call the **unwritten** Commandment of the Decalogue:

"Love your neighbor more than yourself."

Such are these sublime souls who love Christ in their neighbor in such a way that they identify Christ with their fellowman:

"Love each other in the same way as I loved you."

This was the case, for instance for Saint Maximilian Kolbe and Mother Teresa of Calcutta - the list is not exhaustive.

But what about those souls who, until the last moment of

---

137 This text which seems to apply to the Celestial Jerusalem is nonetheless often quoted by the believers in the Intermediate Return of Christ as heralding the establishment of the Reign of God on earth. It would be mistaken, however, to think that the principle of analogy cannot apply both to what will happen on earth for a millennium and what shall take place forevermore afterwards in Heaven, since the former is the prefigure of the latter.

138 Love as the touchstone of perfection and the reverse measure of hate.

their appointed time, refused to believe that God is love and to act accordingly? What of them?

They will be left to the misery of their self-centered ego, as fulfillment of their own will, in that endless pursuit of nonexistence which is hell... They will discover what it means to be dead to all hope, inured against all love, with the sole gratification that they made in their own way.

The elect on the other hand will be surprised by God, as the newborn is gratified by the love of his mother, or as the sight of her beloved rejoices the heart of the Shulamite... (These are mere words, for we cannot account for what we do not know yet.)

POSTSCRIPT

Robert Hugh Benson, well-read in Scriptures, has described the End of Time according to their own rules of plausibility. It was easier for him as for me since he did not foresee Endtimes as a curtain-raiser. Eschatology deals with that part of Revelation which is most mysterious, because it is affected by man's use or misuse of his own liberty. Who am I to bring my own version of things to come? But it is mine only insofar as a "bouquetière" arranges the flowers at her disposal which she receives from her suppliers. Data is not conjured here out of fancy, but from reliable sources. How can one fit such facts together without some measure of subjective interpretation? I had to satisfy my own inner logic, insofar as it applies to things not yet settled into that providential vision which is God's alone. Eschatology is that part of Theology which is most problematic. The incentive came for me as a challenge.

The lesson to be drawn from prophecy is, however and paradoxically, the same as to be drawn from history. Man can learn from the future as he does from the past when he is willing to read it through the eyes of Faith. What is it that shapes the destiny of mankind for the better or the worse, if not its willingness to team up with God or with Satan respectively in the practice of virtue or the pursuit of evil? There have been reformers for the Church as there have been masters of iniquity for the world. That is why a Lenin, once decrepit with age, confided in a moment of lucidity that

197

another Francis of Assisi would have been more beneficial to Russia. "There are many antichrists," according to Scripture, and, may we add, just as there are many "alter Christi" (other Christs). As far as the latter are concerned, according to St. Grignion de Montfort, let us pray Heaven for these "apostles of the End Times." While the Antichrists configure the world to the image of their father, the Devil, is it not appropriate that today it is the Virgin who, in her many apparitions, prepares us for the second Advent of her Son? The lack of awareness of this saving grace of hers, on the part of many Churchmen, is, at least partly, at the source of the present falloff from Faith. With a few exceptions such as that of John Paul II, we do not respond with joy to the prospect of the return of Christ. Better late than never! There is so much to be done.

In 1956 already, at Amsterdam, our Lady of all Nations, had requested in a Message to Pope Pius XII:

"The proclamation of Mary Co-redemptrix, Mediatrix and Advocate should be made before 1960."[139]

What better way of imploring her assistance than by thus praising the Lord for his Providential ways?

Should we not mean what we say when we pray?

The answer seems obvious, but it is not.

Should we believe all we read in the Bible?

The answer to this question is even less obvious.

In both cases, usage has imposed, now and then, formulations which run against the grain of Belief or Revelation.

Thus, when we pray "and lead us not into temptation," we mean the opposite of what we are saying. We mean, "Do not

---

[139] *Les Messages de la Dame de tous les peoples.* Ed. Pierre Téqui, Le Roc Saint Michel, France, 2006, 52e message, 31 Mai 1956.

let us fall into temptation."

And when we read that "God hardened the heart of Pharaoh," we know that this is not the case. God, indeed, does not harden hearts.

That is why there are many texts in which we look for a hidden meaning, and with good reason. It is the spirit that "signifies" and not the letter.

The underlying meaning in the words of the Our Father creates more dilemmas than meet the eye.

Requests two and three of the Our Father are those we tend to take for granted when we neglect to reflect fully on their implication:

"Thy Kingdom come, Thy Will be done on earth as it is in Heaven."

What do we mean by "Kingdom"? – This is where spirits are divided.

Just as the "Will of God" is only too often assumed to be such that it can only be accomplished "in Heaven" and not "on earth."

Justifiably for our purpose, the early Church Fathers and medieval mystics such as St. Bonaventure, plus contemporary visionaries (Lucia of Fatima or Luisa Piccarreta) are of a different persuasion... including the Virgin in her more recent apparitions.

The Kingdom of God is not only meant to be "within us" when the Holy Ghost abides in us, but in society at large; and this is the hope we entertain, comforted by the prophecy of Apoc 20, 4-6, announcing the Reign of "Christ [for] a thousand years."

Indeed, the "signs of the times" are such today that we cannot deny them.

May we recite the "Our Father" with the full compunction of conviction!

We are not praying for something impossible, but eminently desirable.

Let us not fall into the pessimism of a Luther claiming God makes impossible demands as to confuse men into anxious perplexities!

Should we not rather take the prophetic part of the *Magnificat* as the proclamation of things that will take place on earth before their transcendent accomplishment in Heaven?

"He has chosen might with his arm,

He has scattered the proud in the conceit of their heart,

...He has given help to Israel, his servant, mindful of his mercy-"

On this theme, there are two schools of thought.... whose differences are less clearly defined than meets the eye, dealing with the interpretation of Apoc. 20, 4-6: "And I saw thrones, and men sat upon them.... [who] will reign with [Christ] a thousand years."

How close are we to this Reign is also a matter of conjecture...and such is part of this book because its content is mostly prophetic. In this perspective we say with St. Paul: "Do not neglect the gift of prophecy," for fear we should lose hope. But let us confide in Providence whose designs, registered in the Scriptures, are for the pure of heart.

LIST OF ILLUSTRATIONS

Albrecht Dürer, p. 88

12) The four horsemen of the Apocalypse (Apoc 6, 1-8), Albrecht Dürer, p. 122

13) "And the stars of the sky fell to the earth as the fig tree sheds its winter fruit when shaken by a gale ..." (Apoc 6, 13), Albrecht Dürer, p. 134

14) The opening of the seventh seal with the falling of the star named Wormwood and the eagle saying, "Woe, woe, woe to the inhabitants of the earth!" (Apoc. 8-9, 3), Albrecht Dürer, p. 140

15) St. John devouring "the scroll" (Apoc 10, 8-11), Albrecht Dürer, p. 150

16) The Angels restraining the four winds (Apoc 7, 1-9), Albrecht Dürer, p. 156

17) "And I saw an angel ... having the key of the abyss and a great chain in his hand. And he laid hold on the dragon, the ancient serpent, who is the devil and Satan, and bound him for a thousand years. And he cast him in to the abyss..." (Apoc 20, 2-3), Albrecht Dürer, p. 176

NOTA – I am indebted to the Germanisches Museum of Nürnberg for the Dürer woodcuts; to the Akademie der Bildende Kunst in Vienna for the Hieronymous Bosch Last Judgment; to the Hôtel Dieu of Beaune (France) for the Last Judgment by Rogier van den Weyden; & to F. X. Guilberg and O.E.I.L. for the picture of the Virgin of the Escorial. To these institutions, I am deeply grateful.

ABOUT THE AUTHOR

Jacques Cabaud was a professor at the Gustav Siewerth Academy where he taught Church history. He is considered an expert on the life and work of Simone Weil and has published a number of seminal works on her. He has also published a book on contemporary Marian apparitions that has appeared in three languages. He lives in Erlangen, Germany.

Other works by Jacques Cabaud in English:

Simone Weil, A Fellowship in Love (Harvill Press, London, 1964, 394 pages, & Channel Press, New York): out of print, also in its French, German and Mandarin versions.

Is Mary Appearing Today? (Goodbooks Media, Corpus Christi, Texas, 2018, 342 pages): available also in French (2003) and German versions (2016).

www.ingramcontent.com/pod-product-compliance
Lightning Source LLC
Chambersburg PA
CBHW030818270326
41928CB00007B/790